EFFECTIVE RETENTION
OF TITLE CLAUSES

EFFECTIVE RETENTION OF TITLE CLAUSES

JOHN PARRIS
LLB (Hons), PhD

COLLINS
8 Grafton Street, London W1

Collins Professional and Technical Books
William Collins Sons & Co. Ltd
8 Grafton Street, London W1X 3LA

First published in Great Britain by
Collins Professional and Technical Books 1986

Distributed in the United States of America
by Sheridan House, Inc.

British Library Cataloguing in Publication Data
Parris, John
Effective retention of title clauses.
1. Commercial law—Great Britain
I. Title
344.106′72   KD1650

ISBN 0-00-383074-8

Typeset by V & M Graphics Ltd, Aylesbury, Bucks
Printed and bound in Great Britain by
Mackays of Chatham, Kent

Contents

upheld conditional sales – The *Romalpa* case – The *Romalpa* retention clauses – The issues in the *Romalpa* case in the High Court – Did the retention of title clause create a charge on the company's book debts? – *Romalpa* in the Court of Appeal – The accountants' reaction to *Romalpa* – The *Borden* case – Criticisms of *Romalpa* in the *Bond Worth* case – The fallacies of the *Bond Worth* case – An 'artificial concept'?

contract? – The battle of the forms – Ensuring that retention of title clauses are a term of the contract – Identification of the goods – Injunctions against receivers – The presumption of legitimacy – Voidable title of goods – The Cork Report and retention clauses – Presentation of a petition for an 'administrator' under the Insolvency Act 1985 – After the appointment of an 'administrator'

Preface

'A maze if not a minefield'

In 1982, Granada published a book written by me under the title *Retention of Title on the Sale of Goods*. At that time, following the House of Lords decision in *McEntire and Maconchy* v. *Crossley Brothers Ltd* (1895) and the Court of Appeal decision in the *Romalpa* case (1976) the position was relatively simple. If the seller of goods retained ownership of them until he got paid, the courts would give effect to the plain contractual provisions of the parties.

In recent years, however, as Mr Justice Staughton has aptly said, the law on this topic has become 'a maze if not a minefield'.

It was, therefore, not possible for me to revise my earlier book. I have therefore had to restructure it entirely and try to provide a guide through the maze and some indication of how to avoid the mines which lie in the path of businessmen who would like to get paid for goods they have delivered.

The present position is due to two factors.

The main one is that unwarranted concessions against the interests of their clients have been made by counsel in numerous cases on this subject. As Lord Justice Robert Goff said in *Clough Mill Ltd* v. *Geoffrey Martin* (1984):

'The decision in any particular case may have depended on how the matter was presented to the court and, in particular, may have depended on a material concession by counsel. So this is a field in which we have to be particularly careful in reading each decision in the light of the facts and the issues before the court in question.'

The second factor is that there is provision in the Companies Acts for a receiver to seek directions from the Chancery Division of the High Court. Chancery judges in such cases have not given due weight to the express provisions of the contracts and the statutes, and decisions have tended to favour money lenders. The law as it stands in England does no credit to the erudition of either the Bar or the judiciary; the paramount duty of both is to give effect to what the parties have actually agreed.

However, provided careful attention is paid to the terms of a retention of title clause, it is possible to make it effective. This is the purpose of this book.

I am indebted to a number of people who have read the script, and commented upon it – in particular, Malcolm London BSc (Econ), FCA, a senior partner at Cork Gully, and Dr R.R. Pennington, Professor of Commercial Law at Birmingham University – but, of course, the responsibility for the text is entirely mine. I am also grateful to Mr A. Kaufman, MA LLB, solicitor, for allowing me to reproduce, from a lecture, his comments about 'hiving down' [1.04].

John Parris

Chapter 1

The Need for Retention Clauses

1.01 Licensed larceny

At four o'clock one afternoon a wholesaler delivered a large consignment of canned goods to a supermarket. Twenty minutes later an accountant from a leading firm of insolvency practitioners arrived and announced that he had been appointed receiver and manager by the clearing bank which had given an overdraft to the company which owned the supermarket. The agreement for the overdraft had included a document which granted a 'floating charge' [8.07] to the bank over all the assets of the supermarket.

The receiver 'hived-down' [1.03] all assets of the supermarket to a new 'off-the-peg' company [1.04] and sold off the business as a going concern. Amongst the assets he sold off were the canned goods the wholesaler had supplied on credit.

The Inland Revenue got paid. The bank received a substantial portion of what it had lent. The receiver got his share of that, his fees being charged on the amount he recovered. The more he got for the bank, the more he got for himself or his firm. The wholesaler, an unsecured creditor, got nothing at all.

Morally, it is difficult to distinguish that situation from theft. Legally, the difference is that the supermarket has become the owner of the canned goods and they were therefore their property, even though they had not paid a penny for them. As a result, the bank, the secured creditor, and the receiver were both enriched by the wholesaler's loss of his property, property for which he had paid or had to pay his suppliers.

Similarly, shoe manufacturers supplied an old customer, a multiple retailer with a chain of shops. To their surprise, one day they saw a whole page advertisement in the local paper offering their branded goods for sale to the public through the mail at prices far below those charged to their customer. It was the first intimation they had that a receiver had been appointed to the retailers by a secured creditor, a bank.

Liquidation of the retailers followed, as is almost inevitable in these circumstances, and the shoe manufacturers received nothing by way of dividend in the subsequent liquidation for their unpaid goods; the secured creditors took all the assets. Insult was added to injury when the shoe manufacturer's markets were eroded by the sale of their branded goods to the public at less than the cost of production.

This is a not uncommon experience for manufacturers and suppliers of goods. In the *Bond Worth* case [1.05], for example, some £550,000 of Acrilan supplied by Monsanto, and on hand in various forms on the carpet manufacturer's premises, was utilised to satisfy the claims of the debenture holders, Alliance Assurance Co. Ltd.

Not surprisingly, businessmen are tired of supplying goods on credit to companies, only to find these goods seized without payment by a receiver for some secured creditor, usually a bank.

1.02   A 'raw deal' for unsecured creditors

Lord Justice Templeman said in the Court of Appeal in *Borden (U.K.) Ltd* v. *Scottish Timber Products Ltd and Ano.* (1979):

'Unsecured creditors rank after preferential creditors, mortgagees and holders of floating charges, and they receive a raw deal.'

He instanced the case of *Business Computers Ltd* v. *Anglo-African Leasing Ltd* (1977) which he had tried as a High Court judge, where he said:

'The background facts are simple and depressingly typical ... By commercial misfortune or administrative ineptitude B.C. Ltd lurched into insolvency and the debenture holders appointed a receiver. B.C. Ltd's assets are about £1 million. The Crown, the rating authorities, and other preferential creditors take £300,000. The debenture holders take the rest: about £700,000, in part discharge of bank loans, no doubt consisting of capital and interest at the crippling rates of between 10 per cent and 20 per cent which the banks assert they are compelled to charge all and sundry. The trade creditors, who perforce extended some credit to B.C. Ltd in the ordinary course of business, and other unsecured creditors, claiming in all some £3 million, will get nothing.'

He added:

'The question whether in this day and age, it is necessary or desirable to permit the Crown and the holders of future floating charges the totality of the priorities which can be exercised under the existing law is not the subject of debate in this court, though I am inclined to think it is at least debatable elsewhere.'

In the *Clough Mill* case [2.01] and [8.10], the Master of the Rolls interrupted leading counsel for the appellants who was developing this aspect of the matter, by saying: 'But that's a jury point'. Justice and fairness may well be 'jury points' and Sir John Donaldson's observation is a useful reminder that courts are supposed to decide cases on the law and not the merits. However, it is surely preferable that where two possible interpretations of a contract are possible, the one that does not represent 'a raw deal' to one party should be preferred. As will be seen that is not what has happened in all the retention of title cases in English courts.

It is to seek some protection against receivers and liquidators that manufacturers and suppliers in the United Kingdom are increasingly making use of retention of title clauses in the terms and conditions in which they do business. Such clauses have long been familiar elsewhere in Europe and are recognised by all commercially advanced legal systems.

In its simplest form such a clause merely provides that the buyer shall not become the owner of the goods until the seller has been paid. For example:

'Unless the Company [seller] shall otherwise specify in writing, all goods sold by the Company to the purchaser shall be and remain the property of the Company until the purchase price is paid in full.'

'All goods remain our property until paid for in full irrespective of any subsequent sale to a third party'.

But, as will be seen from the examples provided in Chapter 3, there are considerable variations.

1.03 'Hiving down' operation by a receiver

English law provides, as Lord Justice Templeman implied, advantages for banks and financiers. However extravagant their interest rates and however much their claim consists of unpaid interest on unpaid interest, by the term of their debentures, floating charges or secured overdrafts, they scoop the pool of assets in priority to all unsecured creditors.

The position of the latter is further prejudiced by the current practice of many receivers and liquidators, on taking possession on their appointment, of 'hiving down' all company assets to a new and independent company. The receiver acquires an 'off-the-peg' £100 nominal shareholding limited liability company, adopts a trading name similar to that possessed by the original company, and then assigns or otherwise transfers to this new company all the assets, including goodwill, possessed by the insolvent company. These assets include goods delivered but not paid for. The new company is thus enabled to carry on the business without the inconvenience of meeting the debts of its predecessor.

Since the unsecured creditor's only claim is against the company with whom he contracted, he is left with a claim against an empty shell from which all the crab meat has been skilfully extracted. Receivers, of course, claim that by hiving down it is more likely that the business will be continued and sold as a going concern, and that it is only by this method that tax losses can be preserved for the benefit of the ultimate purchaser. But this is scant comfort to unsecured creditors.

1.04   The conjuring trick

As a solicitor, Mr A. Kaufman said in a lecture delivered for the German Chamber of Industry and Commerce in the United Kingdom and numerous German cities:

> 'The receivers will sell the assets only and will usually not include the debtors in the sale.
>
> The exercise is known as a "hiving down" operation and is something which continually baffles my German clients since to the outside world and indeed to the company's suppliers and customers it appears as if the company is continuing in business with the same or similar name, address and directors but mysteriously declines responsibility for payment of its old debts.
>
> What, then, actually happens? It is, in fact, extremely simple. The receivers form a new company into which they transfer or hive down the assets of the old company or such assets which they consider to be saleable.
>
> Very often this new company with all the useful trading assets of the old company, but without any of its liabilities and with such of the former employees as will be required by the purchasers of the new company, is in fact purchased by the previous shareholders, or by the previous management.
>
> They will also purchase from the receivers the goodwill of the old company, namely its list of customers and suppliers, half-finished contracts and, most important of all, the right to use the old trading

name of the old company or if that trading name has been tarnished due to the financial difficulties, the right to use a similar name.

Thus the phoenix rises from the ashes, a conjuring trick which is perfectly permissible under our present law, which allows companies to be formed with no minimum capital and in practice imposes no penalties or punishment on directors who have been involved in a company in receivership or liquidation, and unless real fraud has been committed imposes no personal liability upon such directors ...

The receivers have now sold the assets of the company, will collect in the debts, will pay the proceeds from the sale to their client, the bank – after, of course, collecting their percentage – and the company which by now is just a shell with only liabilities will be placed into liquidation.'

Not surprisingly, he asked: 'What can the poor German exporter do?' The poor British supplier can likewise ask the same question.

1.05   An example of a 'hiving down' operation

In re Bond Worth (1979) was an application to the Chancery Division of the High Court for a direction by joint receivers appointed by the Alliance Assurance Co. Ltd under trust deeds which created floating charges over all the assets as security for debenture stocks in carpet manufacturers, Bond Worth Ltd. Earlier, another receiver had been appointed by the National Westminster Bank Ltd.

Acrilan Fibre had been supplied by the first respondents, Monsanto Ltd, to Bond Worth Ltd for several years but from 1976 all such supplies had been made under a standard contract of sale to which reference will be made later. The clause reserved the equitable and beneficial ownership of Acrilan fibre supplied by Monsanto to Bond Worth until all outstanding indebtedness of Bond Worth to Monsanto had been discharged. The clause further provided that if before payment was made in full, the Acrilan fibre was used in the manufacture of carpets and they were then sold by Bond Worth, Monsanto's equitable and beneficial interest in the fibre would extend to the proceeds of sale.

The National Westminster Bank's receiver went into possession on 16th August 1977. At that date there was owed to Monsanto, for Acrilan delivered to Bond Worth or one of its subsidiaries for which Bond Worth was liable, the sum of £587,397 in respect of twenty-nine deliveries of Acrilan.

Although no accurate stock seems to have been taken by the receiver, there appears to have been in the possession of Bond Worth:

£110,000 of unprocessed Acrilan
£282,000 of yarn made 99.26% from Acrilan
£163,000 of finished carpet stock in which the Acrilan yarn, dyed, formed the substantial part, apart from the latex backing.
There was a total, therefore, of £555,000 of Monsanto's goods.

The bank's receiver was told by telex on the day of his appointment that all Acrilan on Bond Worth's premises was subject to a retention of title clause.

The business of Bond Worth Ltd was hived down by the receiver, with effect from the close of business on 16th August 1977, to a £100 company with no assets, Glixcroft Ltd. No actual stocktaking of Bond Worth's assets was made by the first receiver appointed by the National Westminster Bank on that day.

The hiving down agreement was made on 19 August 1977 between that receiver on behalf of Bond Worth Ltd, whereby Bond Worth agreed to sell and Glixcroft agreed to purchase as at, and with effect from, the close of business on 16th August 1977, and free from all liens and charges and incumbrances, the goodwill, undertaking and all other property and assets of Bond Worth, except for a number of stated categories. Amongst the categories so excluded were 'goods supplied to the vendor under retention of title'.

Mr Justice Slade said:

'The Acrilan which had been delivered to Bond Worth by Monsanto before Mr Milnes' receivership, and which was at the date of his appointment in various stages of manufacture was used by Glixcroft after that date in the manufacture of carpets.'

He also added:

'Believing it was not legally possible to sell to Glixcroft goods which were subject to retention of title, Mr Milnes stated in the course of a meeting (with Monsanto Ltd) that he would transfer to Glixcroft Ltd all goods used in the business excluding those subject to retention of title.'

The judge was asked by the summons to decide the question as to whether, and if so when, Glixcroft Ltd acquired title to the £555,000 worth of Acrilan, in various forms, on the premises of Bond Worth. He regarded that question as irrelevant in the light of his findings, but others may regard it as extremely relevant. How and when did Glixcroft Ltd acquire title if the receiver had expressly excluded from the transfer to that company any goods subject to a retention of title clause, or what he thought was a retention of title clause? The question as to the validity of the clause is not one of law but of the identity of property acquired by the new company. There was no specific sale or assignment to Glixcroft of ascertained goods. What goods were then transferred to them?

On 27th August 1977 the receiver appointed by the National Westminster Bank was supplanted by two receivers appointed by the debenture holders, Alliance Assurance Co. Ltd. Mr Justice Slade said:

'There was not and never has been any entry or other reference in the books of Bond Worth to stocks of Acrilan or goods made from Acrilan withheld from the sale of assets under the hive-down agreement and remaining in the possession, control or disposition of Bond Worth.

Furthermore, no such stocks of goods existed physically, in the sense that there were no Acrilan or goods made from Acrilan separately marked, stored or otherwise set apart from the other assets of Bond Worth, which were sold to Glixcroft.

The Acrilan and Acrilan-derived products so transferred to Glixcroft were all used and disposed of by Glixcroft in the normal course of its business being the continuation of the business previously carried on by Bond Worth.'

The result was that all the assets of Bond Worth Ltd including those goods subject to a specific clause, reserving beneficial ownership to the unpaid sellers until payment, were extracted from the company and transferred to another company for no consideration. As will be seen in due course, Mr Justice Slade – then a chancery judge – for specious reasons, approved this dubious transaction.

1.06 Is 'hiving down' lawful?

The question has not yet come before the courts as to whether the transfer of valuable assets in the company to which the receiver has been appointed to a £100 company with no assets whatsoever apart from two issued but possibly not paid for shares is a lawful operation.

Prima facie the operation appears to be an operation designed solely to defeat creditors, and *ultra vires* the powers of a receiver, even if the intention is to obtain for the secured creditor the maximum amount by selling the company as a going concern together with its tax losses.

To sell vast assets to a shell company with no money and no prospect of ever paying for them unless the shell company is itself acquired by some other concern, must surely be a voidable transaction, even if not – as it is submitted – illegal. It is to be hoped that even if the Director of Public Prosecutions will not stir himself, companies who supply goods and are currently being deprived of their goods by this procedure will undertake private prosecutions of receivers. Certainly, the owner of goods who supplies a company to whom a receiver has been appointed and who proposes to hive down will be entitled to an injunction to restrain him from dealing with the goods in this fashion.

The comments of Mr Justice Hoffman in *In re Palmer Marine Surveys Ltd* (1985) dealing with the positions of liquidators, are relevant:

'Where there is evidence to suggest that assets have been transferred to an associated company for inadequate value, creditors should ordinarily be entitled to have the company's affairs investigated by a liquidator who is not merely independent, but can be seen to be independent.'

'The public is frequently astonished by the ease with which unsuccessful businessmen appear to be able to transfer the assets, goodwill, premises and employees of an insolvent company to a pristine entity with which they continue trading as before, leaving their creditors unpaid.'

'That may be the price to be paid for the entrepreneurial incentive of limited liability; but in cases in which it appears to have happened, thorough investigation is required.'

1.07   Reservation of ownership

The only way a supplier of goods can protect himself is to ensure that a clause is included in the contract of sale which reserves his ownership of the goods until such a time as he has been paid for them.

Such clauses have been used for many years in Germany and Holland and to a lesser extent in France, and there are dozens of decisions upholding them, in all their numerous varieties and permutations, from the courts of those countries. In England, such clauses have always been possible, as will be seen, but businessmen did not appreciate properly the possibilities of such clauses until the *Romalpa* case [5.03] in the Court of Appeal in 1976. In spite of that a few companies, such as Courtaulds, have had retention of title clauses for many years – 'long before Romalpa was in rompers', as their solicitor puts it. It was their standard clause which was used in the *Clough Mill* case [4.03]. Although there were no financial links or connections of any kind between Clough Mill Ltd and Courtaulds, the former had adopted ('cribbed' would be a better word) Courtauld's wording.

Since only £1000 was at stake, Clough Mill were not disposed to challenge the finding of a Circuit Judge sitting in the Manchester Chancery Court that the clause was ineffective because it constituted an unregistered security. However, Courtaulds had a vested interest in upholding the virtues of the clause and they sponsored the appeal. At one time, to support another person's action in this fashion was known as the crime and tort of 'maintenance'. Happily, it is no longer a crime or a tort where the person financing the action has some interest in the outcome, as Courtaulds clearly had in this case.

Chapter 2

Transferring Ownership in Goods

2.01 Property, title and ownership

In discussing ownership of goods, two words are commonly used by lawyers: one is '*the property* in the goods', the other is '*title* to the goods'. The first is said to be all the rights of ownership which can be asserted against the world at large; the second is generally believed to be the rights that pass between seller and buyer.

English law regarding the sale of goods was codified by Sir William Chalmers in the Sale of Goods Act 1893, now replaced, with only minor alterations, by the Sale of Goods Act 1979. Sir William's work has generally been regarded as a highly skilled and satisfactory enactment. However, it does not appear to use the word 'property' in the sense given above, since sections 16 to 20 of the original Act were grouped together under the heading 'Transfer of Property as between Seller and Buyer' and sections 21 to 26 as 'Transfer of Title'.

'Ownership' is a layman's word. The Oxford English Dictionary defines it simply as 'the fact or state of being an owner' and an owner is defined as 'one who owns or holds something as his own; a proprietor; one who has the rightful claim or title to a thing'. As Lord Justice Goff said in *Clough Mill Ltd* v. *Geoffrey Martin* (1984):

'*Prima facie* in a commercial document ... "ownership" means, quite simply, the property in the goods.' [4.03]

He was dealing with a retention of title clause which provided:

'the ownership of the material shall remain with the seller, which reserves the right to dispose of the material until payment in full for all the material has been received by it in accordance with the terms of this contract or until such time as the buyer sells the material to its customers by way of *bona fide* sale at full market value'.

However, in a contract where the words used, in what was clearly intended to be a retention of title clause, were that 'equitable and beneficial ownership' was to remain with the sellers until payment, Mr Justice Slade interpreted this as meaning that legal title should be implied to pass to the buyers and that the sellers would retain only an equitable one: *In re Bond Worth* (1980).

As the Commercial Court judge, Mr Justice Staughton, aptly commented in *Hendy Lennox Ltd* v. *Grahame Puttick Ltd* (1983):

> 'If these words had occurred in a document prepared by commercial men, one might perhaps have concluded that they simply meant ownership.
>
> But this occurred in a document which evidently had a legal provenance and Mr Justice Slade accordingly held that the legal property in the fibre passed to the buyers on delivery.'

This clearly did not accord with the intention of the sellers or, for that matter, the buyers; and therefore disregarded the provisions of section 17 of the Sale of Goods Act 1893, to which his lordship in all his 60,000-word judgment made no reference whatsoever.

In re Bond Worth (1980) merits at least two entries in the *Guinness Book of Records*. It was the longest judgment delivered by any High Court judge. In the Court of Appeal in *Clough Mill* v. *Geoffrey Martin*, the court was invited by counsel for the respondents to read the whole of the judgment. 'What, all 150 pages?' exclaimed the Master of the Rolls, Sir John Donaldson. 'We have other things to do, you know!'

It also contained more errors in law than any other judgment before or since. The first error was the entirely artificial conclusion that what the parties had intended by their contract was that legal title (never mentioned) should pass to intending purchasers while only an equitable title remained in the seller. The second (of many) was that there is such a thing as an equitable title in goods as distinct from legal ownership of them, consisting of 'property' or 'title' in them. The Sale of Goods Act is a comprehensive statute which deals with the only ways in which ownership can pass.

2.02　Equitable and legal ownership

There is a fundamental distinction between ownership of land and ownership of goods. In legal theory, the English Crown still owns every square inch of English soil. As Williams neatly expressed it in his *Real Property* in 1844:

> 'No man is in law the absolute owner of lands. He can only hold an estate in them'.

This means, to lawyers, that when you say you own your freehold house, what you are really saying is that you hold an estate of fee simple in tenure. In practice, of course, it may be virtually the same most of the time as absolute ownership; but in principle it is not. And as a result, there can always be various equitable interest and estates which the courts will recognise, including a 'legal title' and an 'equitable title'.

This distinction between 'legal title' and 'equitable title' goes back to the centuries before the Judicature Act 1873 when three separate courts, King's Bench, Common Pleas and Exchequer administered Common Law. In addition there was the quite separate Court of Chancery which arose, as they did, out of the personal but delegated jurisdiction of the monarch, but much later. Petitions addressed to the monarch were passed on to his Lord Chancellor, 'the keeper of the King's conscience'. At first, the Lord Chancellors decided such petitions on the basis of 'equity', i.e. what was fair and right in their own personal view, so that it was said in the 17th Century that 'Equity varied with the length of the Chancellor's foot': in other words, with his sobriety or the state of his digestion. By the late 18th Century, however, equity – the body of law administered in the Court of Chancery – had hardened into as rigid a set of rules as the common law.

One of its principles was to enforce trusts. In a trust, one or more persons is, or are, entitled to the legal title: that is, the title that the common law courts would enforce. But if he or they had undertaken to hold that legal title 'to the use of' or 'in trust for' another, the Court of Chancery would enforce the trust. The owners of the legal title were then said to be in a 'fiduciary' position – that is, they were bound to exercise all their rights and powers for the benefit of the other, as 'the beneficiary' or the '*cestui que trust*'.

Strictly, even in real property law there could only be one title to land and the beneficiaries could only have an equitable *interest* i.e. that which would be enforced only by the Court of Chancery. But lawyers have slipped into the slovenly way of talking of 'legal title' and 'equitable title' in cases where there were trustees who held the title and another or others who were entitled to have their rights enforced by the Court of Chancery.

The Judicature Act 1873 merged all these courts into a 'Supreme Court of Judicature', consisting of the High Court, divided into different divisions, and the Court of Appeal. Common law and the body of rules called equity were to be administered in all courts with the rules of equity to prevail whenever there was conflict. That is substantially the system we have today, which is why a leader writer in *The Times* aptly described it as 'medieval with Victorian trimmings'.

As will be seen later in discussing the intending purchaser under a retention of title clause [6.01], a person can be in a 'fiduciary' position even though he has not expressly agreed to be a trustee.

However, in the case of goods anybody can be the absolute owner of them. It is therefore highly doubtful whether there can ever be such a thing as *equitable ownership* of goods apart from the legal ownership of them. Clearly, there can be equitable *interests* in goods, by way of trusts or charges, but this is not the same thing as 'equitable title' or 'property'.

It is, of course, perfectly possible to create a mortgage of a chattel by the transfer of property in the goods from the borrower to the lender in order to secure a debt: *Keith* v. *Burrows* (1876). Such a transaction is excluded from the definition of Sale of Goods by section 62(4) of the Act. The lender becomes the legal owner subject to an obligation to transfer the title back to the borrower on the repayment. It is what continental lawyers term a 'resolutive' condition. The transaction may be effected by a document in which case, if the borrower remains in possession of the goods and is an individual, *the document itself* may have to be registered under the Bills of Sale Acts 1878 and 1882 [8.09]. But it seems that there is no requirement for such a document or indeed anything in writing: *Flory* v. *Denny* (1852); *Ramsay* v. *Margrett* (1894); *London & Yorkshire Bank* v. *White* (1895).

All this strongly suggests that there is no such thing known to English law as 'equitable' title to goods. There is only one thing, ownership, known either as 'the property in the goods', or 'the title to goods' and there is comprehensive statutory provision in the Sale of Goods Act for the *exclusive* ways in which property can pass, or title be acquired. For Mr Justice Slade, as he then was, to construe the words 'equitable and beneficial ownership' in a commercial document as meaning that by implication the legal ownership had passed to the recipients of the goods can only be viewed as a major error in law, aggravated even more by his subsequent findings that, as a result, it constituted a registrable charge, void as against a receiver. For reasons set out later, even if it were a charge it was neither registrable under section 95 of the Companies Act 1948 [9.03] nor void against a receiver, who is only an agent for the company and bound by all the company's transactions [9.01].

2.03 Contracts of sale of goods

Section 2 of the Sale of Goods Act 1893 provided, as does the same numbered section of the Sale of Goods Act 1979, that:

'(1) A contract of sale of goods is a contract by which the seller transfers or agrees to transfer the property in goods to the buyer for a money consideration, called the price.

(2) ...

(3) *A contract of sale may be absolute or conditional.*

(4) Where under a contract of sale the property in the goods is transferred from the seller to the buyer the contract is called a sale.

(5) *Where under a contract of sale the transfer of the property in the goods is to take place at a future time or subject to some condition thereafter to be fulfilled the contract is called an agreement to sell.*

(6) *An agreement to sell becomes a sale when* the time elapses or *the conditions are fulfilled subject to which the property in the goods is to be transferred.*'

So, a contract which provides that property shall only pass to the intending purchaser on payment to the seller is an 'agreement to sell' and not a sale.

Furthermore, it is perfectly clear that in English law it is open to the seller to impose what continental lawyers term 'suspensive' conditions to the agreement to sell. That is that property in the goods shall only pass to the intending purchaser on the fulfilment of a particular condition, such as payment.

2.04 Title to be passed by owner

English law about the transfer of ownership in goods is substantially different from those systems of law which are based upon Roman law. These include most European systems, and Scottish law.

In English law there is no provision for acquiring title to goods by undisputed possession for a specific period, although title to land can be acquired in this fashion. If the bicycle that was stolen from you twenty years ago at Oxford can be identified, you are still the owner; an innocent possessor of it, even if he reasonably believed he was the owner because he had paid for it, will lose it. Nor does there in English law have to be a delivery of goods and taking possession of them for ownership to pass.

The fundamental assumption of English law is that nobody who is not himself the owner of goods can make any person who buys from him the owner. This is expressed in the legal maxim *'nemo dat quod non habet'*; i.e. 'a man cannot give what he has not got' – a principle women discovered long before the law did.

This is quite different from Roman law and from most European laws which derive from it. But English law provides many exceptions to the principle. These are relevant when a buyer comes into possession of goods subject to a retention of title clause under which the seller remains the owner and then the buyer re-sells the goods to a sub-purchaser with or without the original seller's consent.

The common law rules as to whether and, if so, when, the ownership of goods passed to the buyer under a contract of sale were, with some modification, incorporated in the Sale of Goods Act 1893. These rules remain substantially unaltered in the present Sale of Goods Act 1979.

2.05   Exceptions to the general rule

The main exceptions to the rule that only the owner of goods can transfer a title to the buyer are: agency; estoppel (section 21); sales in market overt (section 22); seller in possession after sale (section 24); buyer in possession after agreement to sell (section 25(1)); mercantile agents or factors under the Factors Act 1889; goods taken in distress or in execution; innkeepers under the Innkeepers Act 1878; repairers under the Disposal of Uncollected Goods Act 1952; sales of motor vehicles under the Hire Purchase Act 1964; and the Unsolicited Goods and Services Act 1971. In all these cases, subject to different conditions, a person who has no title to goods can effectively pass a title to somebody who buys them from him. So, too, under the Insolvency Act 1985 can the 'administrator' of a company who is appointed by the court [9.13].

2.06   Title obtained by sub-purchasers

Section 21(1) and subsequent sections of the Sale of Goods Act 1979 create a number of exceptions to the general rule that a person who has no title to goods cannot confer on a third party a valid title to them. It is not proposed to deal with all the exceptions mentioned in [2.05], but only with the particular case of dispositions made which will be affected by a retention clause.

The question, so far as the seller with a retention of title clause is concerned, is whether the goods remain the original seller's property, if the buyer sells on those goods to a sub-purchaser; or whether the sub-sale vests the title in the sub-purchaser.

If, according to the basic rule of English law, no title can be passed by anybody who has no title, the original seller can recover his goods from the sub-purchaser irrespective of whether he has paid for them or not. If, however, the sub-purchaser acquires a title, the original seller has no rights against him.

It is therefore of great importance to see how a sub-purchaser can acquire title to the goods under the Sale of Goods Act even though his seller has none to pass to him because title is retained by the original seller.

2.07   Title by estoppel

Section 21 of the Sale of Goods Act 1979 deals with one circumstance in which a title to goods may be acquired by a buyer from a person who is not the owner and has no title to them. This, like the other cases which will follow, is an instance where the buyer *obtains* a good title rather than that a title *passes* to him. It reads:

> Section 21(1): 'Subject to this Act, where goods are sold by a person who is not their owner and who does not sell them under the authority or with the consent of the owner the buyer acquires no better title to the goods than the seller had, *unless the owner of the goods is by his conduct precluded from denying the seller's authority to sell.*'

There are two aspects to this. An agent with limited authority may appear to a buyer to have unlimited authority. For example, if the owner of goods entrusts them to somebody else to sell for him but not under £1000 and that person sells them at a lower price, the buyer will normally get a good title. An agent is only an agent if he has the actual authority of his principal; but he may also have what is called 'ostensible authority'. The principal is bound by his agent's ostensible authority on the principle set out in the italicised words of section 21 quoted above.

To lawyers this is known as 'estoppel'. If the owner of goods holds somebody out as the agent to dispose of them, he is 'estopped' from denying that person's authority to sell them.

The other aspect is to be seen where the true owner allows some other person to appear to the world as if he were the owner. An illustration is to be found in *Stoneleigh Finance* v. *Phillips* (1955) where the owner of a car who wished to raise money on it by way of a hire purchase transaction signed a document for a finance company which stated that a car dealer had the sole, unencumbered ownership of the car. The true owner was estopped from denying that the car dealer was the owner.

The words of section 21 are regrettably vague and do little to help resolve the problem of whether a seller who passes goods to a buyer with a retention of title clause, who knows that the buyer is going to resell the goods as his own, is estopped from denying that a sub-purchaser has become the owner. In *Commonwealth Trust* v. *Akotey* (1926), a decision of the Judicial Committee of the Privy Council (and not therefore strictly binding on the English Courts), it was said that:

'to permit goods to go into the possession of another, with all the insignia of possession thereof and of apparent title, and to leave it open to go behind that possession ... and upset a purchase of the goods made for full value and in good faith, would bring confusion into mercantile transactions'.

However, that case has been much criticised and was not followed in *Mercantile Bank of India Ltd* v. *Central Bank of India Ltd* (1938).

The position appears to be that to allow a buyer to have possession of the goods, even if it is known by the seller who retains title that the buyer will process and resell them as his own, is not sufficient to estop the seller. But possession plus any *indicium* (or proof) of title will estop the owner. But it was held in *Central Newbury Car Auctions* v. *Unity Finance* (1957) that a motor car log book was neither a 'document of title' under section 1(4) of the Factors Act 1889, nor an *indicium* of title.

Of course, if the seller has consented to the buyer reselling the goods as owner thereof, he will be estopped from denying the fact.

2.08 Title from buyer in possession

Section 25(1) of the Sale of Goods Act 1979 (originally section 9 of the Factors Act 1889, and section 25(2) of the Sale of Goods Act 1893) deals with the position where a person who has bought, or agreed to buy, certain goods obtains the possession of the goods, with the consent of the seller, and sells those goods to a person who receives them in good faith and without notice of any lien *or other right* of the original seller.

A lien is the right of somebody who is not the owner of goods, but is in possession of them, to retain them pending payment of a debt. For example, if a man takes his motor car into a garage for repair, the garage proprietor is entitled to keep it until his work is paid for.

Section 25(1):
'Where a person having ... agreed to buy goods, obtains, with the consent of the seller, possession of the goods ... the delivery or transfer

by that person ... of the goods or documents of title under any sale, pledge or other disposition thereof to any person receiving the same in good faith and without notice of any lien or other right of the original seller in respect of the goods, has the same effect as if the person making the delivery or transfer were a mercantile agent in possession of the goods or documents of title with the consent of the owner.'

The sub-section (2) excludes from the operation of this provision a conditional sale (which is the position where there is retention of title by the original seller) which amounts to a consumer credit agreement for the purposes of the Consumer Credit Act 1974.

The term 'mercantile agent' is defined in section 26, but the effect of the section is that the sub-purchaser obtains a good title to the goods as though the delivery to him were made with the consent of the original seller, the owner.

Where goods are admixed with others, so that an ownership in common is created, section 25(1) will only apply if the 'consent' with which the sub-purchaser is in possession of the goods is the consent of all the owners: *Lloyds Bank Ltd* v. *Bank of America* (1938).

'Possession with consent' for the purposes of section 25(1) is apparently sufficient even if the consent is obtained by fraud: *Du Jardin* v. *Beadman Bros* (1952). But it is uncertain whether 'possession' means possession solely in connection with the seller/buyer relationship or whether possession for a purpose entirely unrelated to a transaction of that nature is covered. It seems inconceivable that if Tom agrees to buy a car from Harry on the understanding that possession and title are not to pass until payment in cash has been made, and then Tom borrows the car from Harry in order to go to his bank to collect the money but disappears with it, Tom can defeat the true owner's title by selling it to an innocent purchaser.

It should be noted that for section 25(1) of the Sale of Goods Act 1979 to operate there must be a delivery or transfer by way of sale etc. Neither a receiver nor a liquidator can obtain title to the goods by virtue of this section. The word 'delivery' is defined in section 61 as meaning 'voluntary transfer of possession from one person to another'. Therefore a receiver or liquidator on appointment does not take 'delivery' within the meaning of section 61.

A person who has taken goods which are subject to a retention of title clause or other condition is a person who has agreed to buy: *Lee* v. *Butler* (1893); *Marten* v. *Whale* (1917). But the wording of section 25(1) appears to be wide enough to cover the situation where a buyer in possession with a retention of title clause in favour of the true owners, sells and delivers to a sub-purchaser: *Hendy Lennox (Industrial Engines) Ltd* v. *Grahame Puttick Ltd* (1983).

2.09 Sub-purchaser in good faith

Section 25(1) only confers title where the sub-purchaser is one '... receiving the same in good faith and without notice of any lien *or other right* of the original sellers ...'

The Irish case of *re Interview Ltd* (1973) held, under the Sale of Goods Act 1893, that where a sub-purchaser knew that his seller had the goods subject to a retention of title clause by the original seller, he did not buy in good faith so as to get title. Mr Justice Kenny said:

'The effect of [the retention of title clause] was that the ownership and property in the goods remained in the German companies until the goods had been paid for. Thus [the buyers] could transfer the property and ownership in the goods to any person who bought them in good faith and without notice of the claim and right of the German companies.'

He then referred to the statute and section 9 of the Factors Act 1889 and concluded:

'Interview cannot rely on the Act of 1889 or the Act of 1893 to validate the transaction as a sale because they did not receive the goods in good faith, and they had notice of the rights of the original sellers, the German companies, in respect of the goods.'

It is submitted that the judgment in that case is correct on that point (but on that point alone).

It would appear, therefore, that a sub-purchaser who knows of the retention of title clause in favour of the original seller cannot obtain a good title under this section from a buyer selling with or without the consent of the owner.

2.10 The time when the property passes

In all retention of title cases, the goods are specific, identified and delivered to the intending purchaser. The paramount rule, therefore, is that contained in section 17 of the Sale of Goods Act 1979:

17—(1) Where there is a contract for the sale of specific or ascertained goods the property in them is transferred to the buyer at such time as the parties to the contract intend it to be transferred.

(2) For the purpose of ascertaining the intention of the parties, regard shall be had to the terms of the contract, the conduct of the parties and the circumstances of the case.

Section 19(1) is also relevant:

19—(1) Where there is a contract for the sale of specific goods or where goods are subsequently appropriated to the contract, the seller may, by the terms of the contract or appropriation, reserve the right of disposal of the goods until certain conditions are fulfilled; and in such a case, notwithstanding the delivery of the goods to the buyer, or to a carrier or other bailee or custodier for the purpose of transmission to the buyer, the property in the goods does not pass to the buyer until the conditions imposed by the seller are fulfilled.

Nothing could be more explicit that it is perfectly open to a seller to impose a condition on the sale of his goods that the intending purchaser shall not become the owner until payment.

2.11 Presumptions as to intention

However, section 18 of the Act lays down no less than eight rules for ascertaining the intention of the parties when the parties have not indicated their intention with sufficient clarity.

These rules are relevant to the situation where goods subject to an initial retention of title clause by the seller owner are later combined with other goods or are sold on by the intending purchaser with the authority of the seller. Examples will be given under the chapter dealing with admixture of goods [7.01 et seq.]

It is therefore necessary to deal with these statutory principles as to the presumed intention of parties. The fact that the price remains unpaid or that the seller has given credit does not affect these presumptions.

The presumptions in section 18 are dependent on there being no indication in the parties' agreement or other circumstances of the transaction which make 'a different intention' appear. These days, the courts readily incline to finding a different intention and are reluctant to hold that the property to goods passes to a buyer who has yet to pay for them or take delivery. In *R.V. Ward Ltd* v. *Bignall* (1967), the defendant agreed to buy two cars for £850 and having left £25 in cash went to his bank to get the balance. On the way, he changed his mind. In the course of the judgment, the presumption in section 18, rule 1, to the effect that property passes to the buyer when the contract was made, was discussed. Lord Justice Sellers expressed the opinion that the property had not passed to the buyer. The fact that the buyer had:

> 'agreed to buy two vehicles ... and paid £25 in cash at the time goes but a little way to establishing that the parties intended the vehicles then and there to become the buyer's property. There was not even a payment by cheque. The buyer went to his bank to get cash and that was to be handed over ... He had not even seen the log books or inquired of their existence. No mention was made of the removal of the vehicles or their insurance ...'

Lord Justice Diplock having said that section 17 was the governing rule went on:

> 'In modern times very little is needed to give rise to the inference that the property in specific goods is to pass only on delivery or payment.'

The title therefore had not passed to the intending buyer.

The presumptions as to passing of title contained in section 18 are, of course, irrelevant where there is an express clause reserving title until payment.

2.12 Specific or unascertained goods?

At common law, the presumption was, in the absence of agreement to the contrary, that the ownership of the goods passed to the buyer when the contract of sale was made, if the goods were specific or identified at that time. In any other cases, ownership passed when the goods were subsequently delivered to the buyer.

Whether the purchase price had been paid, or whether the seller had agreed to allow the buyer credit was irrelevant. Ownership was retained by the seller if payment had not been made only in those cases where the contract of sale expressly so provides.

The Sale of Goods Act 1893, however, modified those rules. The time at which ownership passes to the buyer still depends upon whether the goods are 'specific' or 'unascertained'.

'Specific' goods are defined by section 61 of the 1979 Act. 'Goods' are defined in the same section as:

' "Goods" includes all personal chattels other than things in action and money ... and in particular ... includes emblements, industrial growing crops, and things attached to or forming part of the land which are agreed to be severed before sale or under the contract of sale.'

It is material to note that the words 'personal chattels' as defined in the Bills of Sale Act 1878 include a different definition of goods. Some things therefore are 'goods' for the purpose of the Sale of Goods Act, but not 'goods' for the purposes of the Bills of Sale Acts.

It will be noted that neither are exhaustive definitions.

'Specific goods' are defined by the same section as 'goods identified and agreed upon at the time a contract of sale is made'. The distinction is between specific or ascertained goods, and unascertained goods which may be future goods. In the first the seller only performs his obligations under the contract by delivering the very goods which are the subject matter of the contract. With contracts for unascertained goods, the seller performs his obligations by delivering goods which correspond to the description in the contract.

The Sale of Goods Act 1979 provides that the ownership of unascertained goods cannot pass to the buyer until they are ascertained (section 16). The title to specific goods, on the other hand, can pass immediately after the contract is made if the parties so agree (section 18). Section 16 is a matter of law and is not subject to contrary agreement by the parties.

2.13   The passing of property in unascertained goods

The term 'unascertained goods' may carry one of three possible meanings: namely that the goods have yet to be manufactured or grown by the seller; or, that the goods are purely generic goods (e.g. 100 tons of high tensile steel); or, that the goods are an unidentified portion of a specified whole (e.g. 50 tons out of 100 tons of oil stored at a certain place).

Although the Act does not distinguish between these three kinds of unascertained goods, the rules as to the passing of property and risk necessarily differ in the three cases.

Section 16 lays down the principle that where there is a contract for the sale of unascertained goods, the ownership of the goods cannot pass to the buyer unless and until the goods are ascertained. Section 18, rule 5, then provides that unless a contrary intention is shown, where there is a contract for the sale of unascertained or future goods by description, and goods of that description in a deliverable state are appropriated, unconditionally to the contract, either by the buyer or the seller, with the assent of the other of them, the ownership of the goods passes to the buyer.

Ownership cannot pass until the goods are in a deliverable state. Thus if the seller delivers the goods intended for the buyer to a carrier still mixed with other goods (and therefore still unascertained), ownership cannot pass to the buyer.

Furthermore, ownership cannot pass until identifiable goods have been appropriated under the contract. Thus, in *Healy* v. *Howlett & Sons* (1917) it was held that the ownership of a quantity of mackerel had not passed to the buyer because although the seller had given the railway company, which was to transport a consignment of mackerel, instructions to earmark twenty boxes of mackerel for the buyer, that number of boxes had not been separated from the consignment and so had not been appropriated to the contract.

Moreover, where unascertained goods can only be appropriated to a contract after they have been weighed, measured or tested in order to ascertain the price, the ownership of the goods does not pass to the buyer until this has been done.

In *National Coal Board* v. *Gamble* (1959) coal had been appropriated by the NCB to the contract to supply the defendant with a certain quantity by being loaded on to the buyer's lorry, but it was held that the appropriation was not unconditional until the coal was weighed so as to ascertain the total price payable, and the weigh-ticket had been accepted by the buyer.

For the ownership of unascertained goods to pass to the buyer, not only must the goods be identified and appropriated to the contract by the seller or buyer but also the other party must assent to the appropriation.

Usually it is the seller who makes the appropriation by setting aside or despatching particular goods out of a larger stock in fulfilment of his contractual obligations, and the buyer's assent to the appropriation is shown by his taking delivery of the goods, whether he accepts them as conforming to the contract or not.

The courts have been reluctant to hold that anything less than taking delivery amounts to an assent on the part of the buyer, in the absence of any other express signification of his assent. In *Carlos Federspiel & Co. SA* v. *Charles Twigg & Co. Ltd* (1957) there was an 'f.o.b.' contract. The seller segregated the correct number of items, marked them with the buyer's name and arranged for their carriage by sea and then notified the buyer that all this had been done. Because the buyer had not affirmatively indicated his consent, but had merely acquiesced without dissent in the conduct of the seller, this was held not to constitute an assent.

It is therefore clear that the buyer does not impliedly assent to an appropriation by receiving a notice of appropriation from the seller, however detailed it may be, nor by a carrier taking possession of the goods in order to deliver them to the buyer, unless the carrier is expressly appointed by the buyer to be his agent to give his assent (which is unusual).

On the other hand, express terms of the contract may make the seller the buyer's agent to assent to the appropriation which he makes as a seller, and this will be so if the contract expressly provides that when he has appropriated particular goods to the contract, the seller shall hold them as agent or bailee for the buyer

2.14   Part of bulk goods

The rule, though easy to state, may become difficult to apply when there is a question of ownership of part of a bulk. The passing of property in an entire bulk, a cargo of grain or a tanker of oil, is a matter for agreement between the parties. They can agree that property shall pass either before the buyer takes delivery, on delivery, or at some subsequent date, including the date when payment is made to the seller.

But English law insists that property cannot pass in part of the bulk until that part is separated from the bulk or is otherwise ascertained or identified, as the result of section 16 of the Sale of Goods Act 1979 which reads:

> 'Where there is a contract for the sale of unascertained goods, no property in the goods is transferred to the buyer unless and until the goods are ascertained.'

In other words, in English law, a buyer cannot buy goods until he knows what goods he is buying.

In *re London Wine* (1975) Mr Justice Oliver held that the sale of a specified number of bottles of wine of a particular claret from a wine cellar conferred no title to the goods on the buyer. In that he followed the Court of Appeal in *re Wait* (1927) where Wait bought 1000 tons of Western White wheat ex *SS Challenger*, which was expected to be loaded in December 1925 in Oregon. The wheat was duly loaded in bulk and an invoice for the 1000 tons forwarded to Wait. He subsequently became bankrupt and the court held that he had acquired no property in the wheat since it had never been severed from the bulk or specifically identified.

Much the same happened in *Hayman & Son* v. *McLintock* (1907). A Glasgow flour merchant imported a cargo of flour from the USA and had it in his warehouse when he became bankrupt. One creditor paid for 424 bags of flour and had been given a delivery note which he had presented to the warehouseman, who accepted it prior to the bankruptcy. But the creditor acquired no title in the goods. Said the judge:

'These flour bags were not separately marked, and although doubtless, if the buyer had gone to the storekeeper and had got him to put aside the sacks or mark them or put them in another room, that would have passed the property ...'

2.15 The United States' rule

There is no such rule in the United States, and the manner in which the Uniform Sales Act and the Uniform Commercial Code deal with sales or part bulk there illustrates that ownership in common is by no means inconsistent with the common law.

Section 17 of the Uniform Sales Act provided that no property in goods that were unascertained should pass by the contract of sale, but it further provided that 'property in an undivided share of ascertained goods may be transferred as provided by section 6'. Section 6 of the Uniform Sales Act then provided:

'(1) There may be a contract to sell or a sale of an undivided share of goods. If the parties intend to effect a present sale, the buyer, by force of the agreement, becomes owner in common with the owner or owners of the remaining shares.
(2) In the case of fungible goods, there may be a sale of an undivided share of specific mass, though the number, weight or measure of the goods in the mass, is undivided.'

The Uniform Commercial Code, now in force in most American states, provides, in paragraph 2-105(4):

'An individual share of fungible goods is sufficiently identified to be sold although the quantity of the bulk is not determined. Any agreed portion or such a bulk of any quantity therefore agreed upon by number, weight or other measure may to the extent of the seller's interest in the bulk be sold to the buyer who then becomes an owner in common.'

2.16 Goods on sale or return

Rule 4 of section 18 of the Sale of Goods Act 1979 deals with a situation where there is no sale or agreement to sell but the goods have passed into the possession of the other party on approval, or on sale or return, or as it is sometimes called, 'on consignment'.

> 'When goods are delivered to the buyer on approval, or on 'sale or return' or other similar terms the property in the goods passes to the buyer:
> (a) when he signifies his approval or acceptance to the seller or does any other act adopting the transaction;
> (b) if he does not signify his approval or acceptance to the seller but retains the goods without giving notice of rejection, then, if a time has been fixed for the return of the goods, on the expiration of that time, and if, no time has been fixed, on the expiration of a reasonable time.'

It must be stressed again, that this presumption applies only 'unless a different intention appears' so that it is open to the parties to make quite different provisions in their contracts for the passing of title, e.g. for property not to pass before payment.

Although the section appears to be wide enough to cover the situation where goods are supplied unsolicited, in spite of the inept use of the word 'buyer', the better view is that it has no application unless the recipient has requested the goods.

Chapter 3

Supply of Goods and Materials to the Construction Industry

3.01 Sub-contractors in the construction industry

The supply of materials and goods for building and similar work presents special problems for suppliers who seek to retain title until payment. To start with, many, if not most, of the contracts which have as their object the supply of goods for construction work are contracts for 'work and materials' and not the sale of goods.

The common law provisions which existed before the codification in the Sale of Goods Act 1893, that Act itself, and the current Sale of Goods Act 1979 have no application to these transactions. The distinction was emphasised by the Statute of Frauds 1677, section 17, which later became section 4 of the Sale of Goods Act 1893, and was not repealed until the Law Reform (Enforcement of Contracts) Act 1954 came into force.

Under the Statute of Frauds and section 4 of the 1893 Act, contracts for the sale of goods of the value of £10 or more had to be evidenced in writing before they could be enforced; contracts for goods *and* work were not subject to this provision. If a lift for a building were ordered then the contract would be unenforceable unless it were in writing; if a lift were ordered to be installed by the makers then the contract would be enforceable even though it was entirely oral.

For nearly three hundred years, therefore, there was a sharp distinction drawn between contracts for the sale of goods and contracts for the supply of work and materials and a vast amount of erudition has been dedicated to elucidating this distinction. Not all of this learning would commend itself to logicians. Why the making and supply of false teeth should be regarded as a sale of goods, but the making and supply of a portrait should be a contract for work and material is not immediately apparent to the simple mind, but that is what has been decided by the courts: *Lee* v. *Griffin* (1861); *Robinson* v. *Graves* (1935).

Nor is it immediately apparent why the serving of a meal in a restaurant is the sale of goods but putting a hair dye on a customer is work and materials: *Lockett* v. *A. & M. Charles Ltd* (1938); *Watson* v. *Buckley, Osborne, Garrett and Co. Ltd and Ano.* (1940).

3.02 Sale of goods or work and materials?

Although this part of the Statute of Frauds was repealed in 1954, important consequences still flow from this distinction. For one thing, the implied terms of sections 13 and 14 of the Sale of Goods Acts as to merchantable quality, fitness for purpose etc., do not apply to contracts for work and materials and it is only within recent years that the courts have been willing to imply similar conditions where the supplier works with the materials he supplies. The illogicality of this was stressed by Mr Justice Hallett in the case of *Dodd & Dodd* v. *Wilson and McWilliam* (1946) where veterinary surgeons innoculated the plaintiff's cattle with an injection which injured them:

> 'It seems to me that justice certainly does not require that, by taking on themselves the administration of the substance in addition to recommending and supplying it, the defendants thereby in some way succeed in lessening their liability. It might, of course, increase their liability if their method of administration were improper ... but how can it lessen it?'

In the construction industry case of *Young and Marten Ltd* v. *McManus Childs Ltd* (1968) Lord Upjohn also criticised the distinction that appeared to exist between the obligation of a seller of goods and the supplier of them under a work and materials contract. It was, he said:

> 'most unsatisfactory, illogical and indeed a severe blow to any idea of a coherent system of law ...'

In that case, the House of Lords implied similar terms in a contractor's roofing contract to those in the Sale of Goods Act when the tiles proved to have a latent defect. The House of Lords has since extended this obligation further to cover both work and materials, including the design element, in *I.B.A.* v. *E.M.I. and B.I.C.C.* (1980). To some extent, the Supply of Goods and Services Act 1982 has filled in the lacuna in the law.

Where a supplier is nominated by the architect, and that supplier is to provide goods for the contractor to fix to the building, it is regarded as a sale of goods by the supplier to the contractor: and the ordinary rules for the passing of title therefore apply.

However, where the supplier is to do work as well as supply materials, this is not the sale of goods and there is no intention that the property in the goods shall ever vest in the contractor. The intention of the parties is that when the goods are affixed to the land the property in them shall pass to the owner of the site. They then cease to be chattels and become part of the land [3.05].

One result of this is that not only does the Sale of Goods Act 1979 not apply to this work; the Supply of Goods and Services Act 1982 does not either. The contractor is not at any time intended to become the owner of the goods supplied by a 'work and materials' sub-contractor.

3.03 Passing of title in sub-contract work

Normally there is no contractual relationship between the employer (the building owner) and a sub-contractor.

The consequences can be seen from the case of *Dawber Williamson Roofing Ltd* v. *Humberside County Council* (1979). Humberside County Council entered into a contract with the main contractor for the erection of a school in the standard form of building contract, the Joint Contracts Tribunal (JCT) version of 1963. Roofing work was to be done by the plaintiff company as sub-contractors of the main contractors. These sub-contractors were not nominated by the Council or its architect and the contract they (the sub-contractors) entered into with the main contractor was in the form of contract known as the National Federation of Building Trades Employers/Federation of Associations of Specialists and Sub-contractors, the NFBTE/FASS 'blue form'. That contract made no specific provision for the passing of title in the materials but merely provided that: 'the sub-contractor shall execute and complete the sub-contract works to the reasonable satisfaction of the contractor' (clause 2). It also provided that nothing in the sub-contract should create any privity of contract between the sub-contractor and the employer (clause 3). The sub-contractor was to be responsible for loss or damage to any materials brought on site for the sub-contractor's use until 'such materials and goods have been fully, finally and properly incorporated into the works'.

In November 1976 the plaintiffs delivered to the site for use in their roofing work sixteen tons of Welsh roofing slates. Under the main contract, by clause 30(2) of the JCT 1963 edition, the architect was obliged to include in his interim certificates not only the value of the work properly executed, but also that 'of the materials and goods delivered to ... the works for use thereon ...' Clause 14(1) further provided that 'where materials or goods have ... been included in any interim certificate under which the contractor has received payment, such materials and goods shall become the property of the employer'. Clause 16 of the 1980 edition of the JCT standard form of building contract contains similar provisions.

The value of the sixteen tons of Welsh roofing slates brought on site by the sub-contractors was included in an interim certificate which was paid to the contractor. In January 1977 the contractors went into liquidation. This, under the contracts, had the effect of determining the sub-contractor's contract.

The sub-contractors received no payment for the slates and attempted to collect them. Humberside County Council refused to allow them to do so and subsequently made use of the slates for roofing the school, claiming that they were their property. To whom did the slates belong?

It is surprising that a dispute of this nature ever reached the High Court, since the answer to this question was simple: the slates remained the property of the roofing sub-contractor, Dawber Williamson Roofing Ltd. That company had not sold them to the main contractor and had never intended to do so. Therefore the contractor had no title he could pass to the employer, no matter what his contract with the employer might say: *nemo dat quod non habet* [2.04].

Moreover, the sub-contractors were not a party to the JCT contract and there was no privity of contract of any kind between them and the employers. So, they were in no way bound by the terms of a contract to which they were not parties, even if they knew of its terms: *Scruttons* v. *Midland Silicones Ltd* (1962). It was argued, implausibly, that because by their contract with the contractor they were to be deemed to have knowledge of the terms of the JCT contract between the contractor and the employer the terms of that contract were incorporated in their own by reference. The judge rejected this contention.

The NFBTE/FASS 'blue form' for non-nominated sub-contractors made the position perfectly clear, as did the 'green form' for nominated sub-contractors: 'Nothing on this sub-contract contained shall ... create any privity of contract between the sub-contractor and the employer ...': the proviso to clause 3. The same words appear in NSC/4, for use with the JCT 80 contract (which replaced the 'green form'), in clause 5.2.

It is instructive to consider what the situation would have been if the plaintiffs had been simply suppliers of goods to the contractor. In the absence of any terms or indication to the contrary, the property would pass to the contractor, either at the time of making the contract if the goods were specific and identified, or at latest on delivery [2.02]. The contractor could therefore pass a good title to the employer on payment of the interim certificate, by virtue of clause 14 of the JCT 63 contract, whether he had paid for them or not.

Had the supplier retained title until he was paid, the contractor would be 'a person having ... agreed to buy goods' who had obtained 'with the consent of the seller, possession of the goods' for the purposes of section 25(2) of the Sale of Goods Act 1893. And so, therefore, he could pass a good title to the employer. However, the employer himself would not have been 'the person to whom delivery was made'; and if he, or his agent, the architect, knew that the original seller had retained title, the property would not pass under that section (25(1)) of the 1979 Act. The supplier would therefore still be the owner of the tiles.

From the above, it will be seen that in law there is still an important question to be answered: whether a supplier provided materials under a contract of sale or whether he supplies and installs them, in which case it will be a contract of work and materials.

3.04 The distinction between sale and work and materials

It is not always easy to distinguish between the two in law, as the cases mentioned earlier make clear. But it may be vital. In Australia it has been held that a contract for the supply and installation of a revolving cocktail cabinet which slotted into fastenings on the floor and ceiling was a contract for work and materials: *Brooks Robinson Pty. Ltd* v. *Rothfield* (1951). So also were seats installed in a lecture theatre: *Aristoc Industries Pty. Ltd* v. *R.A. Wenham (Builders) Pty. Ltd* (1965); and a lift installed in a building: *Sydney Hydraulic & General Engineering Co.* v. *Blackwood & Son* (1908). On the other hand, the installation of a domestic heater was held to be a contract of sale: *Collins Trading Co. Pty. Ltd* v. *Maher* (1969).

In England, it has been held that where the method of installation is a minor part of the work the contract is for the sale of goods, so that fitted carpets come in this category: *Philip Head & Sons Ltd* v. *Shopfronts Ltd* (1970).

Formerly, it was said that when 'the contract is such that a chattel is ultimately to be delivered ... the cause of action is for goods sold and delivered': *Lee* v. *Griffin* (1861). But that is no longer a reliable test, and there can be little doubt that if the contract requires the design, fabrication and installation in a building of an air-conditioning plant, for example, it will be a contract for work and materials.

3.05 Affixtures to the realty

Retention of title on building and construction materials is further complicated by the principle that chattels which become permanently affixed to the realty cease to exist as chattels and become part of the land.

Mr Justice Blackburn in *Holland* v. *Hodgson* (1872) said:

> There is no doubt *quicquid plantatur solo, solo cedit:* that the general maxim of the law is that what is annexed to the land becomes part of the land ...'

But the learned judge had to qualify that observation by further comment:

> 'When the article in question is no further attached to the land than by its own weight it is generally considered to be a chattel. But even in such a case, if the intention is apparent to make the articles part of the land, they then become part of the land.
>
> 'On the other hand, an article may be firmly affixed to the land and yet the circumstances may be such that it was never intended to be part of the land and then it does not become part of the land.'

Stone lions resting on the top of the pillars of a gate have been held not to be part of the realty. So, too, have tapestries affixed to a wall. It has been held that an underground pipe, installed with the consent of a neighbour, to effect drainage remained the property of the person who installed it and did not become part of the realty under which it passed.

However, since most goods and materials supplied to a construction site are both securely affixed and intended to become part of the land, as a matter of principle they cease to exist as chattels as soon as they are fixed. A seller with a retention of title clause may therefore have his rights to reclaim the goods defeated as soon as those goods become part of the building, subject to the principles set out below. This will apply not only to such obvious goods and materials as cement or paint but also to substantial plant such as lifts, air-conditioning plants, boilers and heaters.

3.06 Contractual right to detach affixed goods

In theory, this general legal position resulting from the common law can be altered by contractual obligations to the contrary. It is open to a supplier of doors, for example, to stipulate that he shall retain title until payment and that should the contractor to whom he has supplied them have a receiver appointed or go into liquidation, he shall be entitled to enter on the site to remove the doors whether or not they are affixed to the realty. There is no reason, it is thought, why that should not be a valid term *inter partes*, i.e. between the contractor and the supplier. The difficulty from the point of view of the supplier is that there is normally no contractual relationship between himself and the employer, the owner of the building, and the licence to enter would come to an end the moment the contractor ceased to be in possession of the site – as, under the standard contracts, he does in the event of receivership or insolvency. The fact that the contractor has agreed to the removal of doors from the realty can in no way bind the owner of the building. If the owner of the building ordered the doors on those terms, it would be binding on him but the courts have shown little inclination to enforce similar agreements where machinery on hire-purchase has been affixed to the realty.

In *Hobson* v. *Gorringe* (1897) it was held that the owner of goods supplied on hire purchase was entitled to enter on the land and remove his goods which had been affixed to the realty. The terms of hire purchase agreement constituted a licence, coupled with an interest in the land.

There is clear authority for this is in *re Morrison, Jones & Taylor* (1914) where the Court of Appeal held that, under an agreement in which a right to enter the land was reserved, to remove a fixture created an equitable interest which took precedence over later created equitable interests such as mortgages and charges.

Such an equitable right will defeat a debenture holder with a floating charge created after the hire purchase agreement. The right to enter and recover the goods, even affixed goods, takes priority over subsequently created equitable interests, whether the debenture holders are aware of the hire purchase agreement or not: *re Morrison Jones & Taylor Ltd* (1914).

It will not, however, defeat a debenture holder with a legal mortgage of land created after the agreement who has no notice of the hire purchase agreement.

In the case of goods brought on and affixed to the realty after a specific mortgage of land, whether legal or equitable, has been created, these goods become part of the mortgagee's security, even if the mortgageee knew of the agreement: *Longbottom* v. *Berry* (1869): *Meux* v. *Jacobs* (1875). But if there is a floating charge over a company's assets which does not specifically attach to the land until it has crystallised, an owner of goods can remove his affixed goods before the charge has crystallised and if he does so, the charge does not exist over his goods: *re Morrison Jones and Taylor Ltd* (1914).

Plant and business fixtures may readily be presumed as excluded from mortgages and charges over realty by agreement between a company and debenture holders: *Gough* v. *Wood & Co.* (1894).

The position of unpaid sellers who have retained title and whose goods have been affixed to the realty will be identical in all respects with those who own and let out goods on hire purchase agreements.

3.07 Right of entry a registrable interest

The main problem, as has been suggested earlier, is that the usual supplier with a retention clause or sub-contractor who inserts one in his sub-contract has usually no contractual relationship with the freeholder or building owner. He may in some cases, however, be in contractual relationship with the freeholder or building owner if the contract is, for example, a management one or the main contractor is otherwise authorised to act as agent for the building owner. In that case, the question of registration of the equitable interest of the right of entry will arise.

It appears that the supplier or contractor is better off where the land is not a registered title since the right of entry does not have to be registered under the Land Charges Act: *Shiloh Spinners* v. *Harding* (1973).

In the case of registered titles, the right of re-entry has to be registered as a minor interest as the result of section 70(1) of the Land Registration Act 1925. Unless on the register, a purchaser – even with express notice of the re-entry right – will take free from it: *Williams & Glyn's Bank Ltd* v. *Boland* (1980).

But a seller with a retention of title clause can do this simply by entering a caution on the register. In that event, a purchaser is deemed to have full notice of the interest: *Parkash* v. *Irani Finance Ltd* (1970).

A seller with a retention title and a right of re-entry is protected against both receivers and liquidators, even if his equitable interest is unregistered, since neither is a 'purchaser' or 'transferor' of the land. Nor does it come within those charges which have to be registered under Section 95 of the Companies Act 1948 or section 395 of the Companies Act 1985 [8.01 *et seq.*] *Shiloh Spinners* v. *Harding* (1973).

Removal of goods affixed to the realty is probably only effective when (a) the goods can be identified and (b) when they can be removed *salve integre et commode*: in other words intact, in one piece and without damage to the remaining structure. Building suppliers should certainly investigate the possibilities of writing a retention of title clause which, in the event of the appointment of a receiver to the contractor, would entitle them to go on site and remove, say, doors, even if installed.

3.08 Retention and the Joint Contracts Tribunal contracts

In 1978, the Joint Contract Tribunal, the body which is responsible for drafting the Standard Form of Building Contract, issued a formal notice entitled 'Retention of title (ownership) by suppliers of building material and goods'.

'The Joint Contracts Tribunal announces that, through its constituent bodies, it has been informed of the following problem. Some suppliers of building materials and goods are including provisions in their contracts of sale with contractors and sub-contractors under which the supplier retains ownership of such goods and materials after their delivery to the site. The terms on which such retention of ownership is secured appear to vary; but in many cases the passing of ownership to a contractor or sub-contractor is dependent upon payment in full for the relevant materials and goods. It is understood that suppliers anticipate being able to use such provisions to enable them either to repossess the goods and materials if they have not been paid for in full; or to claim against the proceeds of any re-sale.

Some employers (and their professional advisers) are seeking to obtain proof of ownership by the contractor (or through the contractor, by any relevant sub-contractor) before operating the provisions of Clause 30(2) [of the 1963 JCT form]. Moreover, in current tenders some employers are seeking to amend Clause 30(2) by making it a condition of the operation of the valuation provisions in that sub-clause that the contractor provides proof of ownership.

The tribunal has considered this matter to see if there is sufficient substance for the concern being expressed by some employers (and their professional advisers) to justify any change in the existing Standard Form provisions in Clause 30(2) and in Clause 14(1). The tribunal, with the concurrence of its constituent bodies, does not think that any change is desirable, and the main reasons for reaching this decision are set out below:

Reasons for decision by Tribunal not to amend Clause 30(2) and Clause 14(1)

(1) A requirement on the contractor to prove ownership of on-site materials and goods could raise serious legal problems, both for the contractor, any relevant sub-contractors and also for the employer (and his professsional advisers). Such a requirement would, therefore, be difficult to meet and so might mean, in practice, that payment for on-site goods and materials would not be operated. Moreover, the obtaining of proof of ownership would add to administration costs as would the checking of such proof by, or on behalf of, the employer. The tribunal concluded that such a requirement would add to the costs of building work by reason of additional administration; and might cause tender prices to rise because contractors and sub-contractors could no longer be certain that materials and goods properly on site would be valued and paid for in interim certificates.

(2) The degree of risk to the employer from not obtaining proof of ownership before paying for on-site goods and materials in interim certificates was not considered sufficiently great to justify the possible additional costs, referred to in (1) above for the following reasons:

(a) The period of risk runs only until such time as the on-site goods and materials are incorporated in the works; from the time of incorporation they cease to be chattels, and any right to repossess by the supplier would be lost. The period of risk is, therefore, from the date of payment by the employer of the relevant interim certificates to the time at which the relevant goods and materials are incorporated in the works; this is unlikely to be more than a relatively short period.

(b) During the limited period referred to in (a), the risk of repossession by a supplier would only, in practice, arise if a main contractor became insolvent. Such insolvency occurs only in a small proportion of the total number of building contracts and this reduces the degree or risk even further.

(c) The Tribunal understands that in many cases the supply contract permits the contractor or sub-contractor to resell the goods and materials. In such cases the supplier's rights are against the proceeds of resale and the supplier has no right to repossess the goods and materials. This reduces the risk to the employer still further.'

3.09 The position of an architect or engineer when certifying

That statement by the Joint Contracts Tribunal merits some comment.

An architect or engineer who is called upon to certify the value of goods supplied or work done for an interim or final certificate under any building contract is liable in contract and in tort to his employer for negligent over-certification: *Sutcliffe* v. *Thackrah* (1974). He is also liable to the contractor in tort for negligent under-certification: *Stevenson* v. *Watson* (1879). Although the Court of Appeal decided in the case of *Chambers* v. *Goldthorpe* (1901) that an architect issuing a final certificate was a 'quasi-arbitrator' and therefore protected from an action by an employer or builder for negligent certification, the House of Lords in *Sutcliffe* v. *Thackrah* (1974) overthrew this principle, although it had been accepted for more than seventy years and was described by Lord Radcliffe in the House of Lords in *R.B. Burden* v. *Swansea Corporation* (1957) as 'established law'. As a result, an architect or engineer who issues a certificate for interim or final payments under a construction contract is not protected in any way for negligent certification.

It is self-evident that he must be liable to his employer if he issues a certificate to the contractor for payment of on-site goods without satisfying himself that the contractor can pass such a title to the employer as will make the employer the owner of the goods for which he has to pay.

In the case of *Ashwell Scott Ltd* v. *Eastlease Ltd* (1980) the plaintiffs secured, with a tender of £624,339, a contract for the construction and equipment of a new computer centre on the Bride Kiln Industrial Estate at Milton Keynes for Scientific Control Systems Ltd ('Scicon'). They started work in April 1973 on the basis of a 'letter of intent' but the contract, in the terms of the Model Conditions of the Institute of Mechanical and Electrical Engineers (1966 edition) was not signed until 2nd July 1973.

The Milton Keynes Development Corporation undertook to act as 'architects, surveyors and engineers' for the project, as agents for Scicon.

On 21st October 1973 they gave Ashwell Scott seven days notice to get off the site, which was complied with. The contractor therefore, in a case named *Ashwell Scott Ltd* v. *Scientific Control Systems Ltd: Milton Keynes Development Corporation, Third Party* (1979) sued for damages for breach of contract and for a *quantum meruit* for work done and materials supplied of £327,033. Scicon brought in the Development Corporation, their 'architects, surveyors and engineers' as a third party and claimed a full indemnity should they be found liable.

After a sixteen-day hearing of that case, Judge Fay QC, sitting on Official Referee's business, ruled on three preliminary points. He held that the expulsion of Ashwell Scott from the site was not a valid exercise of the power to determine the contract contained in clause 12 of the Model Conditions. He held that Ashwell Scott had not repudiated the contract. He also held that by their expulsion from the site, Scientific Control Systems Ltd had been guilty of a wrongful repudiation of the contract.

In the course of the hearing, it emerged that there was an ingenious arrangement between all the parties whereby the air-conditioning to be installed was leased from Eastlease Ltd, the leasing subsidiary of the Norwich Union, with the benefit of 100% write-off against corporation taxation as 'plant', while at the same time constituting 'new build' and therefore zero-rated for the purposes of VAT. At the same time, the engineer was to include it in the certificates he issued to Scicon for payment to the contractors.

Questions about the ownership of those goods were canvassed in front of the judge, and the effect of sections 25(1) of the Sale of Goods Act 1893, the Finance Acts and the Bills of Sale Act were all discussed. He decided that title had passed by estoppel when the air-conditioning was incorporated in the building on the analogy of section 21(1) of the Sale of Goods Act 1893.

He held there had been no binding contract whereby Eastlease Ltd had undertaken to buy the goods from Ashwell Scott.

'The arrangement made ... related only to the mode of payment of Scicon's debts.'

It was in connection with this that he made the remark:

'An engineer who includes in a certificate goods which are not the property of the contractor does so at his own peril.'

In the particular circumstances of this case, no doubt the employer would be estopped from complaining that the engineer was negligent in issuing certificates for goods, the title for which he well knew was not intended to pass to his employer. And, of course, the judge held that the property had passed when the air-conditioning became incorporated in the realty.

However, the architect who included the slates in his interim certificate in *Dawber Williamson Ltd* v. *Humberside County Council* (1979) for loose goods could have no such defence, since he had not satisfied himself that the contractor had a title to pass to the employer.

It is not surprising therefore that architects are unwilling to include goods brought on site in interim certificates without proof that the contractor can pass ownership of the goods to the employer. Clearly they do so at their peril, if the contractor should become insolvent before the goods are affixed.

3.10 The 1985 amendment to JCT 80

However, by 1985, the Joint Contracts Tribunal had second thoughts about the matter and then issued an amendment to the Standard Form.

The amendment attempts to reverse the decision in *Dawber Williamson Roofing Ltd* v. *Humberside C.C.* (1979) by providing new sub-clauses to clause 19.4 of JCT 80, namely 19.4.1, 19.4.2.1, 19.4.2.2, 19.4.2.3, and 19.4.2.4, that every sub-letting shall be subject to terms which are summarised below in connection with clause 21 of NSC/4. This provides:

Clause 21.2.4.3: 'that if the main contractor shall pay the sub-contractor for any such materials or goods before the value therefor ... has been included in any interim certificate – under which the amount properly due to the contractor has been discharged by the employer ... such materials or goods shall upon such payment by the Main Contractor be and become the property of the Main Contractor.'

Clause 21.2.4.2: 'where ... the value of such materials and goods shall have been included in any interim certificate under which the amount properly due to the contractor shall have been discharged by the employer ... such materials or goods shall have been discharged by the employer ... such materials or goods shall be and become the property of the employer and the sub-contractor shall not deny that such materials or goods are and have become the property of the Employer. Provided always that the Architect shall ... have informed the sub-contractor of the amount of any ... payment directed by the Architect ...'

These new terms are to be incorporated in the following JCT standard form contracts:
Private Edition with Quantities
Private Edition without Quantities
Private Edition with Approximate Quantities
Local Authority Edition with Quantities
Local Authority Edition without Quantities
Local Authority Edition with Approximate Quantities;
but not in Scotland
In reality, clause 21.2.4.2 is an attempt to defeat a retention of title clause and the ordinary provision of the standard contracts on a basis of estoppel [2.07]. However, if a sub-contractor himself has no title to the goods because his supplier has retained title, it would appear that the new clause would be entirely ineffective.

3.11 The standard form of building contract JCT 80: suppliers

The 1980 version of the Joint Contracts Tribunal's standard form gives a restricted meaning to 'nominated suppliers'.
By clause 36.1.2 these terms do not apply unless there has been a prime cost sum in the bill of quantities for these goods or materials – even though the supplier has been named on the bills or there is a sole supplier of such goods or materials.
Clause 36.4 prevents an architect from nominating any supplier unless that supplier is willing to enter into a contract with the main contractor, on a contract which contains eleven terms. One of these is clause 36.4.7 and reads 'that the ownership of materials or goods shall pass to the

contractor upon delivery by the Nominated Supplier ... whether or not payment has been made in full'.

There are a number of conditions which circumscribe this discretion of the architect but the most material ones for present purposes are:

Clause 30.3.4: 'where the materials were ordered from a supplier by the contractor or by any sub-contractor, the contract for their supply is in writing and expressly provides that the property therein shall pass unconditionally to the contractor or sub-contractor ...'

Clause 30.3.5: 'where the materials were ordered from a supplier by any sub-contractor, the relevant sub-contract between the contractor and the sub-contractor is in writing and expressly provides that on the property in the material passing to the sub-contractor the same shall immediately pass to the contractor.'

Clause 30.3.6: 'where the materials were manufactured or assembled by any sub-contractor, the sub-contract is in writing and expressly provides that the property in the materials shall pass unconditionally to the contractor.'

Clause 36.4 expressly exempts from the provision that the contractor shall only be obliged to accept nominated suppliers who enter into a contract on the specified terms 'where the architect and contractor shall otherwise agree'. The architect, as agent of the employer in this context, has no power to vary the terms of the contract.

The terms of the contract are silent about what happens if the contractor, through inadvertence or otherwise, accepts the nomination of a supplier who insists on retaining title until payment has been made and who is not willing to enter into a contract whereby the property shall pass upon delivery. The contractor clearly will be bound by the contract he has entered into with the supplier.

All clause 36.4 does is to give him the right to reject a nomination where the supplier retains title until payment. If he accepts it, he will be bound by it.

3.12 The standard form of building contract JCT 80: sub-contractors

There are other forms for use with the standard form of contract between the employers and the main contractor.

What is termed the 'basic method' of appointing sub-contractors is set out in clause 35 of JCT 80. This involves the use of a contract known as NSC/2 between the employer and the sub-contractor, before the sub-contractor has been formally nominated. It authorises the architect to order the sub-contractor before nomination to design and manufacture materials and goods for the work. If the sub-contractor does not get the nomination, the employer undertakes to pay for the design and materials and 'upon such payment, such materials and goods shall become the property of the employer'.

This is the only reference to the passing of title to the goods and the contract is silent as to when property shall pass if the sub-contractor succeeds in becoming nominated. Presumably, it is only on affixture to the realty.

If he is nominated, he is required to enter into a contract with the contractor in the form NSC/4, which replaces the form NFBTE/FASS 'green form' used with JCT 63.

As with the green form, it specifies that nothing contained in the sub-contract documents shall be so construed as to 'create any privity of contract between the sub-contractor and the employer'.

The main JCT 80 contract retains the provisions in clause 30.2 which require the architect to include in his interim certificates not only work properly executed by the sub-contractor but also (by 21.4.12 of NSC/4) 'the total value of the materials and goods delivered to or adjacent to the works for incorporation therein by the sub-contractor ...' Clause 16.1 of JCT 80 again provides that where such material or goods are included in an interim certificate and paid for 'such materials and goods shall become the property of the employer'.

It will be observed that this clause interferes with normal English provisions as to passing of title contained in rule 1 of section 18 of the Sale of Goods Act 1979. That rule reads:

'Where there is an unconditional contract for the sale of specific goods in a deliverable state, the property in the goods passes to the buyer when the contract is made and it is immaterial whether the time of payment or the time of delivery, or both, be postponed'.

Clause 36 substitutes for the passage of title upon delivery. The supplier and the contractor can, of course, displace rule 1 or any other rule by a specific agreement to the contrary. But it would require the agreement of both parties and it would not be affected by an order to deliver say, ten thousand bricks to the site. In that case property will pass not upon delivery but when, in accordance with rule 3, the seller has set aside this quantity of bricks and 'the buyer has notice thereof'. The latter, of course, may be when the bricks arrive at the site but it will not be a term of the contract.

Once again this clause is totally ineffective to pass title to the employer. In the case of sub-contractors providing work and materials, the main contractor has no title to pass to the employer and the sub-contractor is not a party to the JCT 80 form containing these provisions. As in *Dawber Williamson* [3.03], the property in goods and materials brought on site by the sub-contractor, if he actually owns them, remains vested in him until he incorporates them in the building – even if the main contractor has been paid for them. No doubt, if the sub-contractor actually receives payment for them before they are incorporated, the courts would readily assume, in spite of the curious silence of the contract NSC/4 and NSC/4a about this, that it was the intention of the parties that property should pass to the employer.

3.13 Materials off-site

The JCT 80 standard form empowers, but does not require, the architect to include in an interim certificate the value of any material or goods 'before delivery thereof to or adjacent to the Works' provided they are materials intended for incorporation (clause 30.3).

These clauses are specifically aimed at preventing the architect from including in his interim certificates materials off-site for which the original supplier has retained title until payment.

Curiously, these clauses would appear to exclude the architect from including in interim certificates off-site material prepared or obtained by a nominated sub-contractor under 'the basic method', NSC/4, or the 'alternative method', NSC/4a, since neither of these contracts provides that property in the goods shall ever pass to the contractor.

A further requisite before the architect may include off-site goods or materials in any interim certificate is:

Clause 30.3.8: 'The Contractor provides the Architect ... with reasonable proof that the property in the materials is in him and that the appropriate conditions set out in clauses 30.3.1 to 30.3.1.7 have been complied with.'

This being so, it seems strange that the provision in clause 30.3 appears at all in the contract since there can rarely be cases where the condition can be complied with. The clause corresponds roughly to clause 30(2)A, incorporated at a late stage into the JCT 63 contract.

3.14 Other contracts

The JCT 80 standard form of building contract is not the only form in use for building work in the United Kingdom. For work by government departments, it is common to use the GC/Works/1 form devised by the Property Services Agency of the Department of Environment which makes all property of the contractor brought on site the property of the employer authority. Civil engineering work is usually done under the fifth edition of the Institution of Civil Engineers (ICE) contract.

None of these has, as yet, made specific provision for the effect of retention of title clauses so they will be governed by the principles set out above for the standard form.

3.15   A Scottish retention of title case

In Scotland, the Court of Session in *Archivent* v. *Strathclyde Regional Council* (1984) held that title had passed to the employer under section 25 of the Sale of Goods Act where payment for ventilators had been included in an interim certificate but the supplier had retained title. This is manifestly incorrect in that (a) section 25 requires a contract between the supplier and the purchaser, and there was no such contract; and (b) that contract must be 'an agreement to buy goods' and there was no such agreement.

Chapter 4

Types of Retention of Title Clauses

4.01 Simple retention of title clauses

The first class of retention of title clauses is the simple one. These include:

'The ownership of any goods delivered shall remain with us until the full invoice price has been paid.'

'The property in the goods shall not pass to you until payment in full of the price to us.'

'The property in all goods shall remain with us until payment in full has been received.'

'The title in the goods does not pass to our customer until they have been paid in full.'

'Notwithstanding that the buyer or his agent obtain possession of the goods, the ownership therein shall remain in the company (the seller) until such time as payment is made in full to the company.'

'Notwithstanding delivery the property in the goods shall remain in the company until the customer has paid in full therefor.'

'Title of goods supplied shall not pass to the customer until payment has been made of the full contract price.'

'The property in the goods shall pass to the stockist only when the goods which have been delivered to the stockist have been paid in full.'

Problems that may arise with simple clauses are set out below.

4.02 The problems of simple retention clauses

(1) They do not deal with the question of risk of damage or destruction of the goods. Under English law the passing of ownership and risk normally go together. Section 20 of the Sale of Goods Act 1979 provides:

> 'Unless otherwise agreed, the goods remain at the seller's risk unless the property in them is transferred to the buyer, but when the property in them is transferred to the buyer the goods are at the buyer's risk whether delivery has been made or not.'

If title is retained until payment, it is prudent therefore for the seller to provide that the risk shall pass to the buyer on delivery. A seller with a retention clause should therefore either provide by the terms of his contract that the risk passes to the intending buyer on delivery, or himself insure the goods.

(2) These conditions do not give a right, nor does the general law, for the seller to enter on the buyer's premises to repossess the goods. Only an express term of the contract of sale can do this. Often, clauses provide for this, as in the following examples:

> 'Notwithstanding that the Buyer or his agents obtain possession of the goods the ownership therein will remain in the Company (the seller) until such time as payment is made in full to the Company, which shall be entitled to all rights of access to the Buyer's premises to enforce its rights hereunder.'

> 'If payment is overdue in whole or in part the Company (the seller) may (without prejudice to any of its other rights) recover or recall the goods or any of them and may enter upon the customer's premises for that purpose. These conditions constitute authority for any third party authorised by the Company to enter upon any other premises wheresoever the goods are situated for the purpose of recovering the goods or any of them.'

> 'The Company shall be entitled and the Stockist hereby grants to the company a licence to enter upon the premises of the Stockist during normal business hours for the purpose of removing such goods and to remove such goods from the Stockist's premises.'

> 'The Company shall be entitled to enter upon any premises of the customer for the purpose of removing such goods and new products

manufactured with such goods from the premises, with a view to clear any outstanding debt.'

'On termination of the customer's power of sale in accordance with the foregoing conditions, the customer must place the goods and new products manufactured with them at the disposal of the company, which reserves the right to enter upon any new premises for the purpose of removing such goods and new products, such rights to include severance where necessary from realty.'

These rights of entry may be a registrable interest under the Land Charges Act 1925 [3.07].

(3) Such clauses do not specify with sufficient clarity when the owner's right to repossess the goods in default of payment or some other event shall arise. Even words such as:

'If payment of the total price or other sums is not made on the due date' (thirty days after despatch of products) 'the supplier shall have the right with or without prior notice at any time to retake possession of the whole or any part of the products (and for that purpose to go upon any premises occupied by the purchaser thereof) without prejudice to any other remedy of the supplier'

are insufficient. It is essential to specify that the right to immediate repossession shall arise upon the appointment of a receiver. If not, the credit period may not have expired before the receiver is appointed.

(4) Such clauses may, in the case of a buyer who is in possession of the goods who resells them to a sub-purchaser who knows nothing of the retention clause, be defeated by the provisions of section 25(1) of the Sale of Goods Act 1979 [2.06].

4.03 The 'current account' clause

A more sophisticated form of the retention of title clause is one where the property is not to pass until all the other goods sold by the seller to the buyer have been paid for in full. In France this clause is known as a *compte courant* clause, and in Germany as a *Kontokorrent* clause.

At one time in Germany doubt was expressed about the validity of such clauses, since it was contended that the ownership of goods subject to such a clause might never pass to the buyer and it was therefore inconsistent with it being a contract of sale. These doubts were however resolved by a decision of the German Supreme Court as long ago as 1935.

A typical example is to be found in the *Romalpa* case itself:

'The ownership of the material to be delivered by A.I.V. will only be transferred to purchaser when he has met all that is owing to A.I.V. no matter on what grounds. Until the date of payment, purchaser, if A.I.V. so desires, is required to store his materials in such a way that it is clearly the property of A.I.V.'

Other examples seen in the United Kingdom are as follows:

'The property in the products shall remain in the supplier until the payment of the total price thereof and any other payments due to the supplier from the purchaser have been made.'

'Ownership in the goods shall remain with the company until such time as the purchaser has paid in full all that he owes to the Company.'

'Until full payment has been received by the Company for all goods supplied at any time by the Company (1) the property in the goods shall remain in the Company ...'

'Until such time as full payment has been received by the Company for all goods whatsoever supplied all goods shall remain the property of the Company.'

'Notwithstanding delivery of the goods or any part thereof the property in the goods shall remain in the seller until the purchaser has paid the purchase price in full as well as any other payments due to the seller whether hereunder or in respect of any other liability to the seller whatsoever.'

The Court of Appeal, somewhat surprisingly, in *Clough Mill Ltd* v. *Geoffrey Martin* (1984) seems to have gone out of its way, although the matter had not been argued before it, to have approved such clauses.

Mr Justice Robert Goff pointed out that not only:

'property in a delivered parcel of goods was reserved but also this extended until a certain event: *viz*, until payment in full for all the materials received by the buyer ...

The difficulty with the present condition is that the retention of title applies to material delivered and retained by the Buyer, until payment in full for all the material delivered under the contract has been received by the Seller. The effect is therefore that the Seller may retain his title in material still held by the Buyer, even if part of that material has been paid for.'

He highlighted the problems by taking a hypothetical example:

'Suppose that the seller agrees to sell 1000 tons of material to the buyer at £10 per ton. He delivers 500 tons. Of these 500 tons, only 250 tons are paid for by the buyer: so £2500 have been paid, and another £2500 are due and outstanding.'

He then postulated an event which in his view (but, it is submitted, incorrectly) would amount to a repudiation of the contract by the buyer, and continued:

'Of the 500 tons delivered, 300 tons are still at the buyer's premises, unsold and unused, now worth £4000 instead of £3000 as they were at the time of the contract of sale.

Can the seller re-sell the whole 300 tons? And, if he can and does so, does he have to account to the buyer for that part of the price already paid which cannot be appropriated to the 200 tons already used by the buyer in manufacture and so must be appropriated to part of the 300 tons, i.e. £500.

And must the seller account to the buyer for the profit element of £1000 obtainable on the resale (no doubt allowing for any expenses of the sale)?'

His conclusion was that since the property in the whole 300 tons still belonged to the seller, he was entitled to sell them off for his own account, but would be bound to repay the part of the purchase price which had already been paid, subject to a set-off arising from a cross-claim from the seller for damages for repudiation of the contract by the buyer.

It is a highly interesting speculation in the law but has about as much relevance to real life as discussion about how many angels can dance on the point of a needle. An unpaid seller with a current account clause is most unlikely to recover enough of his goods to meet the buyer's obligations.

However, what this erudite discussion does illustrate is that the current account clauses can, and will, be given effect to by the courts.

4.04 The 'continuing retention' clause

These clauses purport to extend the retention of title clause from the buyer to any purchaser from him and provide that any such purchasers shall not get title until the purchase price has been paid. A clause which attempts to do this is:

'Title of goods supplied shall not pass to the customer or to any person claiming under him until payment has been made of the full contract price. In case of non-payment the Company shall be entitled to repossess or trace the goods or the proceeds of sale from the customer or its liquidator or receiver or from any purchaser or other person drawing title from the customer.'

This type of clause is not frequently found in England because there are two serious problems with it:

(1) The English doctrine of privity of contract prevents a person who is not a party to a contract from having obligations imposed upon him by it. Since sub-purchasers are not parties to the original contract of sale they are not bound by such terms, even if they know of them: *McGruther* v. *Pitcher* (1904); *Port Line Ltd* v. *Ben Line Steamers Ltd* (1958). There are, however, numerous exceptions to this, including terms which 'run with the land'. There are certain obligations in relation to land which bind not only the contracting parties but subsequent owners who acquire the land with notice of the terms. It has been suggested that if the goods are identifiable the same principle may apply.

(2) Section 25(1) of the Sale of Goods Act 1979 (previously section 25(2) of the Sale of Goods Act 1893) provides that a sub-purchaser who knows nothing of the retention of title clause will get a good title [2.08].

In other jurisdictions, obligations are imposed on a buyer to include a retention of title clause in favour of the seller in any contracts he makes and to take on an undertaking from sub-purchasers from him that they will impose the same condition on persons to whom they may resell. The same is possible in English law.

4.05 The 'proceeds of sale' clause

This clause authorises the buyer to resell the goods but provides that the proceeds of sale shall be held by him as an agent or trustee for the seller until the price owed by the buyer has been paid. It is supplemented frequently by the provision that the buyer's rights against his sub-purchaser shall be held in trust for the seller and/or shall be assigned by the buyer to the seller on demand. Such clauses are frequently found in England:

'The title in the goods does not pass to our customer until they have been paid for in full and if our customer sells the goods before the goods have been paid for, then we have the right to the proceeds of such sale.'

'In the event of the Buyer reselling or otherwise disposing of the goods or any part thereof before the property therein has passed to him [under the basic retention of title clause] then the Buyer will, until payment in full to the Company [the Seller] of the price of the goods, hold in trust for the Company all his rights under any such contract of resale or any other contract in pursuance of which the goods or any part thereof are disposed of, or any contract by which property comprising the said goods or any part thereof is or is to be disposed of, and any monies or other consideration received by him thereunder.'

'Notwithstanding delivery the property in the goods shall remain in the company [the Seller] until the customer hereby declares itself trustee of the goods for the company until such payment is made and the customer hereby declares itself trustee of the goods for the company until such payment is made and the customer shall hold the goods and any proceeds of sale of the goods and any rights arising from any sale thereof as trustee for the company.'

'Ownership in the goods shall remain with the Company [the Seller] until such time as the purchaser has paid in full all that he owes the Company. Until that time the purchaser shall keep the goods for the Company in its capacity as fiduciary owner, although the purchaser shall be entitled to sell the goods to a third party within the normal carrying on of his business on the conditions that such sale shall be for the Company's account and, if the Company so require, the purchaser shall hand over to the Company any claims emanating from the sub-sale that he has against his buyer.'

'The risk in the goods passes to the buyer upon delivery, but equitable and beneficial ownership shall remain with us until full payment has been received (each order being considered as a whole), or until prior resale in which case our beneficial entitlement shall attach to the proceeds of resale on to the claim for such proceeds.'

'In the event of the buyer reselling or otherwise disposing of the goods or any part thereof before the property has passed to him, the Buyer will, until payment is made in full to the Company [the Seller] of the price of the goods, hold in trust for the Company all his rights under any such contract of sale or other contract in pursuance of which the goods or any part thereof are disposed of, or any contract by which property comprising the said goods or any part thereof is or is to be disposed of, and any monies or other consideration received by him thereunder.'

'The Buyer shall be entitled to sell both the goods supplied by the Seller in their original state or manufactured goods incorporating the goods supplied to third parties subject to the condition that the Buyer so long as it has not fully discharged its indebtedness to the Seller shall pass to the Seller the claims the Buyer has against the third parties or the proceeds of sale of goods to third parties.'

'Subject to the following appropriate clauses, the customer shall have the right to sell the goods and new products referred to above in the ordinary course of business on the understanding that the proceeds of any such sale shall belong to the company to whom the customer shall account on demand.'

This clause raises very many problems, as will be seen in subsequent chapters. They include questions such as:

(1) Whether there can be created contractually an assignment of a future chose in action (i.e. the debt owed by the sub-purchaser to the buyer for the resale of the goods)?
(2) Whether these terms, in the case of a buyer who is not a corporate body, constitute a 'bill of sale' which has to be registered under the Bills of Sale Acts, 1878 and 1882?
(3) Whether these terms in the case of a buyer which is a company incorporated under the Companies Acts constitute a charge which has to be registered within twenty-one days by the company under the Companies Acts.
(4) Whether any of these terms create a valid trust in favour of the seller, or at least a fiduciary obligation?

(5) If the intending purchaser is bailee of the goods of the owner, does he have by operation of law to hold proceeds of sale for the owner?

4.06 The 'aggregation' clause

This clause permits the buyer to use the goods to fabricate other products from them or to incorporate the goods into composite products. It purports to vest the ownership of the resulting composite products in the seller to the exclusion of all other suppliers, or as an owner of the products in common with the buyer and all other suppliers who have reserved similar rights in proportion to the value of the goods supplied by them respectively.

English examples of this type of clause include the following:

'If any of the goods are processed into other goods before payment in full for the goods has been received by the Company [the Seller], the goods including all of any other goods as aforesaid shall be the property of the Company, and the customer hereby declares itself trustee of such goods for the Company until such payment is made, and the customer shall hold such goods and any proceeds of sale of such goods and any rights arising from any sale thereof as trustee for the Company.'

'Should the goods become constituents of or be converted into other products while subject to our equitable and beneficial ownership, we shall have the equitable and beneficial ownership in such other products as if they were solely and simply the goods.'

'The Seller and the Buyer agree that when the goods are manufactured into new objects or are mixed with other goods, or if the goods in any way whatsoever become a constituent of other goods, the Seller shall have the ownership of the new manufactured goods as security for the amount owing to the Seller. The transfer of ownership of the new goods will be considered to have taken place at the moment when the goods supplied by the Seller are converted into the new goods or are mixed with or become a constituent of other goods. Until payment in full is made to the Seller the Buyer shall keep the goods in question for the Seller in its capacity of fiduciary owner and shall store the goods in such a way that they can be recognised as such should the Seller so require.'

'The property in the goods shall remain with the Company [the Seller] in accordance with this Condition and the Company shall be entitled to re-delivery of the goods notwithstanding the subjection of the goods to any admixture or treatment whether by the Stockist or others.'

'Upon determination of the customer's power of sale, the customer shall pass the goods and any new products into which they have been incorporated to the Company [the Seller] in an effort to clear the debt.'

'In cases where the goods or part thereof have been converted into other products, whether or not this involves the addition of any other ingredient or item whatsoever irrespective of the proportions thereof, the conversion shall be deemed to have been made on the Company's [the Seller's] behalf and legal and beneficial ownership of the resulting products shall pass in full to the Company.'

The problems of clauses of this nature in English law are discussed in [7.01 *et seq.*].

Chapter 5

Romalpa and After

5.01 Conditional sale and hire purchase

It has long been possible in English law for the owner of goods selling them to another person to retain title until he is paid. Two decisions of the House of Lords, decided in 1895 but relating to the law before it was codified in the Sale of Goods Act 1893, make this perfectly plain.

The first dealt with a conditional sale – that is, one where there is an agreement to sell with the condition that the property shall pass to the buyer only when he has paid the last of several instalments, i.e. when he has paid the whole of the purchase price.

In June 1892, an Irish cooper called Thomas Peel entered into a contract with Crossley Brothers Limited to acquire a gas engine on terms that the engine should remain the property of Crossley Brothers until Peel had paid in full the price of £240 by instalments.

The material parts of the agreement were:

'BETWEEN Crossley Brothers Ltd ... of Openshaw, Manchester in the County of Lancashire (hereinafter called "the Owners and Lessors") of the one part and Thomas Frederick Peel, cooper of 6 Cathedral Place, Limerick (hereinafter called "the Lessee") of the other part.

The owners and lessors hereby agree to let to the lessee and the lessee hereby agrees to take and hire from the owners and lessors one Otto gas engine ... delivered and fixed complete in Limerick on the following conditions:

The Lessee shall and will pay to the owners and lessors as and for rent for the said Otto gas engine the following sums ... which sums so agreed to be paid amount in the aggregate to the sum of £240 ... and that upon payment by the lessee of the several sums aforesaid then this agreement shall be at an end and the said Otto gas engine shall become the property of the lessee as purchaser thereof for the said sum of £240 so to be paid

as aforesaid but until the said several sums shall have been fully paid ...
the said Otto gas engine shall remain the sole and absolute property of
the owners and lessors.'

Other clauses dealt with care of the engine, marking of it by plates as the
property of the owners, and an undertaking by Mr Peel not to remove it
from the building in which it was installed without notice to the owners.
Specific provisions dealt with failure to make the instalment payments, or
the bankruptcy of the lessee: the balance of the full sum of £240 became
immediately payable and recoverable by the owners

'who, however, instead of seeking to recover such balance may, if they
think fit, seize and resume absolute possession of the said engine
wherever the same may be and for this purpose if necessary may break
into the premises of the lessee where the said engine may from time to
time be or be reasonably thought to be ...'

Mr Peel had paid only one instalment, £60, before he was adjudicated
bankrupt on 30th June 1893.

The issue in the case was the one which is familiar: who owned the gas
engine? Crossley Brothers Ltd applied to the court for an order that it
should be delivered up to them. The judge refused the order. The Court
of Appeal in Ireland ordered the engine to be handed over to the Crossley
Brothers. The appellants appealed to the House of Lords.

5.02 Why the House of Lords upheld conditional sales

In the Court of Appeal, counsel for the assignees argued that the
transaction was caught by the 'reputed ownership' or 'apparent ownership' clause of the then current Bankruptcy Act. The Court ruled against
them on this point. In the House of Lords, that argument was abandoned.

The thrust of the argument for the appellant assignees in the House of
Lords was that the contract was only a 'colourable device' to cloak the true
transaction between the parties; that the real relationship between the
parties was that of seller and purchaser, with the seller having a charge on
the gas engine for the unpaid purchase money. If so, since the charge was
not registered under the Bills of Sale Acts 1878 and 1882, it was void.

These Acts, which are still in force, provide that *documents* recording
mortgages of certain chattels, where the owner remains in possession,
must be registered within seven days of their creation: section 8, Bills of
Sale Act 1882. If not registered, the security is void. The Acts do not apply
to mortgages and charges over chattels which are created by limited

liability companies: *re Standard Manufacturing Co. Ltd* (1891). So the only practical application is where the chattels are owned by an individual who creates a mortgage or charge over them. But where such charges are created by a company, they become registrable under the Companies Acts.

The effect of the Bills of Sale Acts was described by Lord Herschell LC:

'Under the Act where a bankrupt has transferred the property in his goods to another person, or given that person rights in the nature of rights and property over them, if the goods remain in his possession and he becomes bankrupt, his assignees in bankruptcy can claim the goods ... unless the instrument carrying out the transaction has been registered as a bill of sale.'

His lordship then continued:

'But of course, in order to make out that the assignees have a title to this engine under the Bills of Sale Act, *it is absolutely essential to prove that the property in the engine, at some time or other, had passed to the bankrupt.*

If the property never passed to the bankrupt, he can never have conveyed it or signed it, or given the right to seize, or *have given any rights over it within the meaning of the Bills of Sale Acts ...*

Upon an agreement to sell, it depends upon the intention of the parties, whether the property passes or does not pass ...

Here the parties have in terms expressed their intention, and said that the property shall not pass till the full purchase money is paid.

I know of no reason to prevent that being a perfectly lawful agreement.'

Lord Watson supplemented the Lord Chancellor's observation by remarking that:

'It is perfectly plain that the agreement is one of sale and purchase and nothing else.

It does not in the least follow that, because there is an agreement of the sale and purchase, the property in the thing which is the subject matter of the contract has passed to the purchaser.

That is a question which entirely depends upon the intention of the parties. *The law permits them to settle the point for themselves by any intelligent expression of their intention.*'

The other law lords concurred.

The case of *McEntire and Maconchy* v. *Crossley Brothers Ltd* became the foundation upon which the vast expansion of conditional instalment sale agreements, otherwise known as 'deferred sale agreements' or 'suspensive sale agreements' took place, just as the other House of Lords decision, which follows it immediately in the law reports, *Helby* v. *Matthews and Others* (1895) became the foundation of hire purchase transactions. In fact, it can be said that upon these two cases hang all the law and the profits of consumer credit.

The difference between conditional sales and hire purchase is that under the latter contract the hirer has the option to purchase, usually for a trifling sum, after the hiring period, the goods which are the subject matter of the contract. He is not contractually obliged to, nor does the title automatically pass to him when he has paid all instalments. By a conditional sale agreement, property in the goods passes automatically to the buyer when he has paid the full purchase price.

Mr Singer of Singer Sewing Machines is commonly credited with having invented purchase of goods by instalment payments. In England, after numerous abuses of instalment purchasers by hire purchase companies, the law was reformed by the Consumer Credit Act 1974, parts of which only came into force in 1985.

However, the principles laid down in these cases are fully applicable to all retention of title cases. It matters not that the purchase price is to be paid by instalments. If the owner retains property until payment, it is irrelevant in principle whether the price is to be paid by instalments or at one time (apart from some consumer sales subject to the Consumer Credit Act 1974).

5.03 The *Romalpa* case

The full possibilities of the conditional sale did not strike most manufacturers and suppliers until the case of *Aluminium Industrie Vaassen B.V.* v. *Romalpa Aluminium Ltd* was heard in the Court of Appeal in 1976. The case was concerned with the supply by a Dutch company of aluminium foil to an English company. In spite of observations in later cases to the contrary it was clearly the intention of the parties that the foil should be processed into other goods.

It will be necessary to analyse this case in depth in due course but it is sufficient at the moment to say that the capriciousness of English litigation is well illustrated by it.

The retention of title clause used was an inelegant translation from the Dutch. The contract of sale, including the clause, was expressly made subject to Dutch law and actionable only in Amsterdam. Neither counsel raised the issue of foreign law, and neither the High Court nor the Court of Appeal received any evidence of the law of sale applicable in the Netherlands.

The case was (quite incorrectly) decided on the basis that English law applied. In fact, Dutch law at that time and at the moment of writing has substantial differences from English law.

The Court of Appeal, as Lord Justice Templeman said in the *Borden* case:

> 'looked with sympathy on an invention designed to provide some protection for one class of unsecured creditors, namely unpaid sellers of goods.'

Other courts subsequently have been less sympathetic to retention of title clauses. It is submitted that, for the reasons given by Lord Justice Templeman, they ought to be, provided the clauses are properly drafted, although as that judge conceded:

> 'There is no logical reason why this class of creditor should be favoured as against other creditors such as the suppliers of consumables and services.'

Perhaps the answer to that comment is that most suppliers of services, such as solicitors and barristers, already take effective steps to ensure that their services do not go unrewarded. The supplier of goods is rarely able to demand payment in advance.

5.04 The *Romalpa* retention clauses

The case of *Aluminium Industrie Vaassen B.V.* v. *Romalpa Aluminium Ltd* came before Mr Justice Mocatta in the Queen's Bench Division of the High Court of Justice on 3 February 1975 and he delivered a reserved judgment on 11 February of that year, which went unreported at the time. It was not, in fact, reported until the case was heard in the Court of Appeal.

The retention of title clause with which he was concerned read, in the English version of the Dutch original:

> 'Clause 13. The ownership of the material to be delivered by A.I.V. will only be transferred to purchaser when he has met all that is owing to A.I.V. no matter on what grounds.

Until the date of payment, purchaser, if A.I.V. so desires, is required to store this material in such a way that it is clearly the property of A.I.V.

A.I.V. and purchaser agree that, if purchaser should make (a) new object(s) from the material, mixes this material with (an)other object(s) or if this material in any way whatsoever becomes a constituent of (an)other object(s) A.I.V. will be given the ownership of this (these) new object(s) as surety (*sic*) of the full payment of what purchaser owes A.I.V.

To this end A.I.V. and purchaser now agree that the ownership of the article(s) in question, whether finished or not, are to be transferred to A.I.V. and that this transfer of ownership will be considered to have taken place through and at the moment of the single operation or event by which the material is converted into (a) new object(s), or is mixed with or becomes a constituent of (an)other object(s). Until the moment of full payment of what purchaser owes A.I.V. purchaser shall keep the object(s) in question for A.I.V. in his capacity of fiduciary owner and, if required, shall store this (these) object(s) in such a way that – if A.I.V. so desires – purchaser, as long as he has not fully discharged his debt to A.I.V. shall hand over to A.I.V. the claims he has against his buyer emanating from this transaction.'

It will be seen that this in essence falls into three parts: a simple retention of title clause, a current account clause, and an aggregation clause.

5.05 The issues in the *Romalpa* case in the High Court

A.I.V. supplied aluminium foil to Romalpa Ltd until 1st November 1974 when the latter's banker, Hume Corporation Ltd, appointed a receiver pursuant to powers contained in a debenture. The day before the appointment of the receiver, A.I.V. issued a writ against Romalpa and the same day obtained from Mr Justice Cusack an interlocutory injunction restraining the company from disposing of aluminium foil in its possession.

By their statement of claim, A.I.V. sought, *inter alia*:

(i) a declaration that they were entitled to a charge on the sum of £35,152.66 held in an account by the receiver, representing the proceeds of sale of aluminium foil supplied by A.I.V. to Romalpa;

(ii) a declaration that aluminium foil to the value of £50,235 held by the receiver originating in deliveries to Romalpa by A.I.V. was the latter's foil; and an order for delivery up;

(iii) alternatively (and as the judge put it, 'very much as a third string to their claim') judgment for the price.

The receiver admitted holding foil to the value of £50,235 which were deliveries by A.I.V. to Romalpa. In the proceedings, he conceded that A.I.V. were the owners of this unsold foil and were entitled to an order for its delivery up. He thereby agreed that clause 13 was effective to retain the ownership of the foil which actually came into his possession on assuming his office.

As Professor R. R. Pennington observed later:

'This was unquestionably a proper concession, since it has long been established that a receiver obtains no better title to a company's assets than it has itself, and although he is not personally bound by contracts entered into by the company, he can enforce no greater rights under such contracts than the company itself possesses': see [9.01].

The case therefore concerned solely the sum of £35,152.66, the proceeds of sale of foil to various third parties, which sum the receiver had placed in a separate account. He did not dispute that, at the date of his appointment, Romalpa owed A.I.V. £122,230.

So far as the £31,152.66 was concerned, the judge said:

'It is common ground that the effect of the clause is that, whilst money was owing by the defendants to the plaintiffs, any aluminium foil delivered by the plaintiffs to the defendants, whilst still in their possession, was held by them as bailees.

'It is clear therefore that counsel for Romalpa had conceded that, under the clause, the status of Romalpa was that of the bailee of the property of A.I.V.'

In spite of the wording of this last paragraph of clause 13, both counsel were agreed that there was no express authority to sell on unmixed foil and that a term had to be implied into the contract that Romalpa were entitled to do so.

It was argued on behalf of the receiver that once the foil was sold on, the relationship between A.I.V. and Romalpa became purely that of debtor and creditor – with the result that A.I.V. were merely unsecured creditors in the impending insolvency.

Against this, the plaintiffs argued that because the defendants were bailees, it inevitably followed that a fiduciary relationship existed between the parties. The judge explained:

'It was not necessary, said the plaintiffs, to find as a prerequisite of the right to trace an express or constructive trust. The equitable proprietary remedy followed as a consequence of the finding that the defendants were bailees.'

A fiduciary relationship is one between two persons where one is under an obligation to use legal rights and powers in the interest of the other. The relationship of trustee and beneficiary is one such fiduciary relationship, but equity does not require a full formal trust before holding that one person is under a duty to account to the other. It followed that because there was that relationship of bailor and bailee, there was a duty to account to A.I.V. Therefore, equity gave a right to the receipts.

The defendants contended that the equitable right to trace did not apply in the absence of an express or constructive trust. As Professor Goode observed in *The Law Quarterly Review* in 1976:

'The assumption in this line of argument namely that there was no constructive trust to a considerable extent begged the question, for ... a trust relationship of some kind is essential to the right to trace in equity, and in the absence of an actual trust the key issue is whether the relationship between the parties was such as to impose a fiduciary obligation to account for the asset the subject of the claim.'

There are several earlier cases in which a fiduciary relationship has been imposed even where there was no trust. One such is *Sinclair* v. *Brougham* (1914). In that case, a building society operated current accounts at a time when that was illegal. The building society went into liquidation. There were three classes of claimants to the assets. The first were those who had lent money on long term accounts which were lawful. The second class were the shareholders. The third were those who had put their money into current accounts which the building society had no power to operate.

The House of Lords decided that those who had money in the current account were entitled to treat the society as a fiduciary for it, because their contracts of deposit were *ultra vires* the building society and these depositors were not creditors of the society. But they were entitled in equity to be treated as such because the building society, having received their money, had become a fiduciary for them. Everything, therefore, flowed from the admission of Romalpa's counsel that the defendants were bailees of A.I.V.'s goods. Since they were bailees of another's goods, they were in a fiduciary position; since they were in a fiduciary position they were in equity obligated to account to A.I.V. for all the proceeds of the sale of their goods.

The judgment in *In re Hallett's Estate* (1880) was quoted in support of the last limb of that proposition. In it, Lord Jessel MR said:

> 'The modern doctrine of equity as regards property disposed of by persons in a fiduciary position is a very clear and well established doctrine. You can, if the sale were rightful, take the proceeds of sale, if you can identify them.'

In another passage, he made it clear that in this principle there was no distinction between formal trustees and other persons in a fiduciary position.

> 'Has it ever been suggested, until very recently, that there was any distinction between an express trustee, or an agent, or a bailee, or a collector of rents or anybody else in a fiduciary position? I have never heard, until quite recently, such a distinction suggested ... it can have no foundation in principle, because the beneficial ownership is the same, wherever the legal ownership may be.'

Later, Lord Jessel MR dealt expressly with the position of bailees:

> 'Now that being the established doctrine of equity on this point, I will take the case of the pure bailee. If the bailee sells the goods bailed, the bailor can in equity follow the proceeds ... Therefore there is no difficulty in following the rule of equity and deciding that in a case of mere bailee ... you can follow the money.'

Mr Justice Mocatta held that clause 13 created a fiduciary relationship and not just a simple debtor/creditor relationship and, therefore, the plaintiffs were entitled to the relief they sought.

5.06 Did the retention of title clause create a charge on the company's book debts?

Mr Justice Mocatta also dealt with another point in the words:

> 'A further point made by counsel for the defendants was that if the plaintiffs were to succeed in their tracing claim this would, in effect, be a method available against a liquidator to a creditor of avoiding the

provisions establishing the need to register charges on book debts; see section 95(1)(2)(e) of the Companies Act 1948.

He used this only as an argument against the effect of clause 13 contended for by counsel for the plaintiffs. As to this, I think counsel for the plaintiffs' answer was well founded: namely, that if the property in the foil never passed to the defendants, with the result that the proceeds of sub-sales belonged in equity to the plaintiffs, section 95(1) had no application.'

This issue is discussed in detail in a subsequent chapter [8.01 *et seq.*].

5.07 *Romalpa* in the Court of Appeal

In the Court of Appeal, counsel for Romalpa was allowed to amend his notice of appeal to raise other issues. Judgment was given on 16 January 1976.

It then appeared that the sales to sub-purchasers had been made by the receiver and that he had kept those receipts separate from others. Said Lord Justice Roskill:

'There was no suggestion that the sub-sales were other than authorised by the plaintiffs or that the sub-purchasers concerned did not acquire a valid title to the several quantities of foil'.

This represented two further substantial concessions by counsel for Romalpa.

Lord Justice Roskill held that the only question before the Court of Appeal was:

'whether there was a fiduciary relationship between the plaintiffs and the defendants which entitles the plaintiffs successfully to claim these monies'.

Unlike Mr Justice Mocatta, he did not base his answer to this question on the concession by counsel that Romalpa were bailees of the goods, but upon his construction of the terms of clause 13.

Discussing the contention that the contract simply resulted in the normal relationship of the creditor/debtor, he said:

'Clause 13 plainly provides otherwise. The plaintiffs as sellers were to retain the property in the goods until all - and I underline *all* - that was owing to them had been paid. It is obvious that the business purpose of the whole of this clause, read in its context in these general conditions, was to secure the plaintiffs, so far as possible against the risk of non-payment after they had parted with possession of the goods delivered, whether or not those goods retained their identity after delivery ...

In the case of unmanufactured goods, this was to be achieved by the plaintiffs retaining the property until all payments due had been made...

The burden of counsel for the plaintiffs' argument was, first, that all goods dealt with in pursuance of clause 13 were, until all debts were discharged, the plaintiffs' goods which the defendant were authorised to sell on the plaintiffs' behalf and for the plaintiffs' account but only within the framework of clause 13. Since the goods were the plaintiffs', the defendants remained accountable to the plaintiffs for them or for their proceeds of sale, so long as any indebtedness whatever remained outstanding from the defendants to the plaintiffs. Hence the creation of the fiduciary relationship on which counsel for the plaintiffs sought to rely.'

Lord Justice Roskill then dealt with the fact that the first part of clause 13 did not authorise Romalpa to sell on unprocessed the goods which were the property of A.I.V., nor did it prescribe what was to happen to the proceeds of sale if such goods were sold.

'It was common ground at trial and during argument in this court that some implication had to be made into the first part of clause 13; since, otherwise, the defendants could not lawfully sell the manufactured goods in their possession, at least until they were paid for – for, as already pointed out, they were the plaintiffs' and not the defendants' goods.

To hold otherwise, as I think both parties accepted, would be to stultify the whole business purpose of these transactions.

What, if any, implication is to be made beyond that?

The first part of clause 13 is silent not only as to the power of sale, but as to the dealing with any proceeds of the goods lawfully so sold by the defendants.

Is the admitted power of sale ... fettered or unfettered? If it is fettered, is the fetter that, so long as any indebtedness remained outstanding in any respect from the defendants to the plaintiffs, the defendants after a sub-sale remained accountable to the plaintiffs for all proceeds of sub-sales, not even as counsel for the defendants pointed out in argument, being able to retain for themselves the profit on any such sales?'

In addition to clause 13, hitherto mentioned, the contract contained two other clauses which Lord Justice Roskill considered of importance. He said:

Clause 25: 'Should purchaser remain in default of any payment for which he is liable to A.I.V. then A.I.V. is entitled to stop all deliveries, irrespective of which contract with purchaser they spring from, and to rescind the contract in question without judicial intervention, all this without prejudicing their right to full compensation and without prejudicing their right to take back at once from purchaser the material by virtue of what is laid down under 13 is still their property'.

Clause 22: 'Payment has to be made nett cash by purchaser not later than fourteen days after the date of invoice preferably by payment by transfer to the postal giro or banking account of A.I.V. If required, a bill of exchange can be drawn. The place of payment for all deliveries is Vaassen (Gld). This also holds good when a bill is returned unpaid. In spite of any complaints about flaws in the material delivered, purchaser is obliged to pay the purchase price at the time laid down.'

Clause 22 had been varied subsequently allowing 75 days' credit.

Counsel for Romalpa relied upon that latter clause. As Lord Justice Roskill said:

Counsel for the defendants relied much on the 75 days credit though, as I have already ventured to point out, the problem is the same whatever the length of the credit.

But the longer the period it can be fairly said the greater the business, if not the legal force of this part of counsel's argument.

If the plaintiffs were right, counsel for the defendants argued, then whenever sub-purchasers paid the defendants before the 75 days credit had expired, the defendants could not use those proceeds in their business for any purpose whatever save for paying their creditors, the plaintiffs; they must always retain those specifically for the plaintiffs' account and pay them over to the plaintiffs unless and until the entirety of outstanding indebtedness was discharged.

This, he said, would deprive the defendants of all day to day finance and, so far from according with business efficacy would produce precisely the opposite result, for it would cause acute cash-flow problems, and make conduct of the defendants' business impossible.

This is a formidable argument if one looks at the matter solely from the point of view of the defendants. But this matter has to be regarded in the light of the contractual provisions agreed on by both parties, and the question of business efficacy, in relation to which there are here obvious competing business considerations, must be answered in the light of what both parties expressly agreed upon and therefore must be taken also impliedly to have agreed on, and not unilaterally from the point of view of one party only.'

He then concluded that there was, as both counsel agreed, an implied power of sale, and that:

'one must imply into the first part of the clause not only the power to sell but also the obligation to account in accordance with the normal fiduciary relationship of principle and agent, bailor and bailee.

Accordingly ... I find no difficulty in holding that the principles in *In re Hallett's Estate* ... are of immediate application and I think the plaintiffs are entitled to trace these proceeds of sale and recover them.'

With that, Lord Justice Goff agreed, expressing the view that it was 'a short question of construction'. He concluded: 'The power of sale to be implied where none had been expressed must be qualified so as not to defeat the intention clearly shown by clause 13 as a whole, including the latter part, which only emphasises this ...

The implied power must, therefore ... be a power to sell, not for the defendant's own account but for the account of the plaintiff, unless and until all monies owing be paid.'

5.08   The accountants' reaction to *Romalpa*

The Romalpa case created a great deal of interest amongst executives of manufacturing companies and wholesalers. At the same time, it was received with hostility by accountants, especially those who had remunerative practices concerned with insolvency, and by the money lenders, including the banks.

The argument of the latter was that the decision weakened the position of secured creditors and therefore was likely to result in restricted lending. They then stimulated and financed a concerted assault on all the propositions of law which had been authoritatively enunciated by the Court of Appeal, on the basis of English law as it had been established for centuries and approved by the highest court in the land, the House of Lords.

The Council of the Institute of Chartered Accountants, in association with other bodies, issued a guidance statement about retention clauses. In essence, its advice was to ignore them:

'In drawing up the accounts of undertakings trading on terms whereby goods are supplied subject to a reservation of title, it is necessary to decide at what stage they should be treated as sold by the supplier and purchased by the party to whom they are supplied ("the customer").

In reaching this decision, it is considered that the commercial substance of the transaction should take precedence over its legal form where they conflict. The substance of transactions of this nature has to be decided from consideration of all the surrounding circumstances.

The circumstances surrounding the transaction may indicate that the reservation of title is regarded by the parties as having no practical relevance except in the event of the insolvency of the customer. The goods concerned may be supplied and payment for them may be due in a manner identical with other goods which are not subject to a reservation of title.

In such circumstances, where the customer is a going concern, it is considered that the omission of the stock (or, if resold, the debtors) and of the corresponding liabilities from the balance sheet of the customer would prevent it from showing a true and fair view of the state of affairs.

Similarly, the accounts of the supplier would also be distorted by the omission of such goods from sales and debtors. Accordingly, *it is recommended that in such circumstances the goods should be treated as purchases in the accounts of the customer and as sales in the accounts of the supplier.*' (Author's emphasis)

However, they did add that the accounts should disclose:

'the fact that certain trade creditors might in an insolvency be in a position to obtain payments of the amounts due to them ahead of the holder by a floating charge and [the existence of these] unsecured creditors would normally need to be disclosed if such amounts were material.'

5.09   The *Borden* case

The first retention of title case to come to court after *Romalpa* was that of *Borden (UK) Ltd* v. *Scottish Timber Products Ltd.* Judgment was delivered by Judge Rubin QC, sitting as a deputy judge of the High Court, on 15 November 1978. The facts are outlined in [6.09] and the present author considers that the trial judge was totally right in law and logic. However, he was reversed by the Court of Appeal for reasons that are set out in [7.01].

5.10   Criticisms of *Romalpa* in the *Bond Worth* case

Before the Court of Appeal considered the appeal in the *Borden* case, however, Mr Justice Slade, then a judge in the Chancery Division of the High Court, had taken upon himself to deliver a detailed criticism of the decision of the Court of Appeal in *Romalpa*, by which he was, of course, supposed to be bound.

His voluminous judgment was delivered on 12 February 1979, after a case which had occupied the court's attention for thirteen days, starting on 1 December 1978 and concluding on 17 January 1979.

By the time the Court of Appeal came to consider the *Borden* appeal, *Bond Worth* had not been reported, but the lords of appeal were supplied with copies and it clearly influenced their minds.

The facts of this case are set out in [1.05].

Having concluded that legal title had passed to the buyers with each delivery of Monsanto's goods – a conclusion which was entirely unjustified by the terms of the contract or the Sale of Goods Act 1893 – Mr Justice Slade then went on to hold that all the sellers had retained by the use of the words 'equitable and beneficial ownership' was a mere equitable title.

It has already been pointed out [2.02] that there is no such thing so far as goods are concerned. There is either property or title, i.e. absolute ownership.

Mr Justice Slade then went on to hold that, since the purpose was to secure payment, this constituted a charge *created by the buyer* and was therefore void against other creditors for non-registration under section 95 of the Companies Act 1948. These findings will be considered later in detail [8.01 *et seq*].

However, he still had to overcome the obstacle that Bond Worth Ltd were bailees of Monsanto's goods and therefore were liable to account in a fiduciary capacity for the proceeds of sale, as clearly had been laid down by the Court of Appeal in the *Romalpa* case, which he was found to follow. He went on therefore to say:

'All three judgments seem to have accepted that there was no conceptual difficulty in the proposition that, as between itself and its sub-purchasers, the defendants sold as principal, but that as between itself and the plaintiffs, those goods it was selling with its implied authority from the plaintiffs were the plaintiff's goods, which it was selling as agent for the plaintiffs, to whom it remained fully accountable.'

Mr Justice Slade should have known, as Mr Justice Mocatta and the three experienced judges in the Court of Appeal knew, that there were no conceptual difficulties in the proposition that Romalpa could sell on, both as agents for A.I.V. and as principals on their own account. What he found difficult is a well-recognised principle of English commercial law exemplified in numerous cases about commodity and stock jobbers. The comment of Lord Roskill, as he now is, with respect summarises the position accurately, as do the comments of Professor Goode in *The Law Quarterly Review*, already quoted [5.05].

Mr Justice Slade went on to say:

> 'For the purpose of my present decision, therefore, it is perhaps unfortunate that the decisions in *Ex parte White, Foley* v. *Hill* and *Randell's* case do not appear to have been quoted in argument before either court in the *Romalpa* case.'

These cases will be considered subsequently [6.03] but it can be said now that none of them would have in any way influenced the Court of Appeal to arrive at a different decision.

He then advanced his extraordinary proposition that any bailment requires a return to the bailor 'of the identical subject matter in its original or altered form'. That merits detailed examination of the nature of bailment, and the right to trace the proceeds of bailed goods [6.01 *et seq*]. Possibly, Mr Justice Slade in the Chancery Division had never heard of conditional sales or hire purchase transactions. In these there is no doubt that the recipients of the goods are bailees for the owner and that the intention of all the parties is that the goods bailed should never return to the bailor 'in its original or altered form'. Even Roman law in later periods recognised a bailment where the goods were never intended to be returned to the owner but were in due course to become the property of the bailee.

5.11   The fallacies of the *Bond Worth* case

It is greatly to be regretted that Mr Justice Slade's judgment in *In re Bond Worth* was not appealed. The sum at stake would have well justified an appeal even to the House of Lords. His judgment contained many elementary errors in law.

They included:

(1) The incorrect interpretation of the written contract in that the retention of 'beneficial and equitable ownership' in no way implied that legal title had passed to the prospective buyers.

(2) Holding that there could be separate equitable ownership of goods and legal ownership in defiance of the Sale of Goods Act which clearly lays down the circumstances in which title, i.e. absolute ownership, shall pass [2.02].

(3) Ignoring the provisions of the section 17 of the Sale of Goods Act in that title to goods should pass when 'the parties to the contract intend it to be transferred'. Neither buyer nor seller ever intended that property should pass to the prospective buyer on delivery of the goods and the written contract made no such provision.

(4) Holding that an intending purchaser could not sell both on his own account and as agent for the unpaid supplier [5.07].

(5) Holding that the retention of title clause constituted a charge on the goods.

(6) Holding that the charge was *created by* the intending purchaser – a quite extraordinary contention, in view of the *Romalpa* case.

(7) Even more extraordinary was the conclusion that there could be no bailment of goods in English law unless it was intended that the actual goods in their original or altered form were to be returned to the bailor [6.01 *et seq*].

(8) Holding that there could not be a bailment where the bailee was authorised to process the goods into a different form.

(9) Holding that even if it were a charge, it was not an unpaid seller's lien, which did not require registration under the then Companies Act 1948 [8.06].

(10) Holding that the charge was registrable under section 95 of the Companies Act 1948, without specifying in which of the three classes it came [8.01 *et seq*].

(11) Holding that a receiver was not bound by the contracts entered into by the company [9.01].

5.12   An 'artificial concept'?

Unfortunately other lawyers have been misled into following Mr Justice Slade's contentions. Professor P. S. Atiyah, in the seventh edition of his book *The Sale of Goods* (1985), wrote about the *Romalpa* case.

'The result was in many respects extremely artificial, because the decision of the Court of Appeal involves the conclusion that all the money received by the defendants from the sale of the goods had to be held on trust for the plaintiffs, including even the profit made by the defendants from making and reselling the goods.

Had the plaintiffs strictly enforced their right to have this money paid into a separate bank account, therefore, none of it would have been available for use by the defendants (except to pay the plaintiffs). It is very unlikely that the parties actually contemplated that the money would be used in this way: clearly the plaintiffs did not want to interfere with the daily business activities of the defendant, they merely wanted to be able to step in when the defendants' financial position became precarious and then seize hold of whatever could be found.

Furthermore, the equitable ownership of the proceeds of sale which the plaintiffs claimed, and which the Court of Appeal upheld, was also artificial. Obviously, if these proceeds had actually exceeded the sums due to the plaintiffs nobody intended that the plaintiffs could keep the excess.

This fact alone demonstrates that what was really involved here was a mortgage or charge, since the plaintiffs were only entitled to the proceeds of sale insofar as they were necessary to pay off what was due to them. But that conclusion would have involved recognition that the arrangement was registrable under the Companies Act as the grant of a mortgage or charge; and yet this was not the outcome of the case, partly because the question was not even argued in the Court of Appeal.

The *Romalpa* case itself is therefore a somewhat unsatisfactory authority.'

Professor Atiyah, without justification, described the *Romalpa* case an 'ill considered' decision. He concluded:

'To summarise: a reservation of title clause is effective so far as the original goods are concerned so long as they retain their identity and remain in the possession of the buyer. But attempts to extend the sellers' preferential rights (a) to other goods made with the goods sold, or (b) to the proceeds of sale of the goods of the buyer, are at present highly vulnerable to attack as unregistered charges. So long as the *Romalpa* case remains overruled however, (which may well mean, only so long as the point does not reach the House of Lords), it may be possible to avoid the requirement of registration by a carefully worded clause which stresses that the "buyer" is not really a buyer but a bailee, which insists that the bailee is only entitled to use the goods to manufacture other goods as a trustee, and on behalf of the seller, and which provides that the proceeds of such sale of goods (or the original goods) are to be held on trust in a separate bank account. Furthermore, if the intention of the parties is that the so-called bailee is to have the residuary right (in the nature of an equity redemption) to any balance of the proceeds of sale after payment of the price of the goods (and other goods, supplied by the seller, if the clause so provides), then the whole clause will probably fail, because this will demonstrate that the transaction is really a mortgage, or charge and not a genuine bailment.'

The professor, however, backed the wrong horse. The Court of Appeal, as has been seen [1.01, 1.07, 2.01, 4.03] in the *Clough Mill* case, rejected these arguments.

The present position therefore can be summarised:

(1) A retention of title clause which reserves ownership to the supplier [4.01] until payment does not constitute a registrable charge under the Companies Act.
(2) A 'current account clause' [4.03] is equally valid.
(3) The 'proceeds of sale' clause [4.05] is likely to be upheld by the courts.
(4) Although there are comments in *Clough Mill* that the 'aggregation clause' [4.06] may possibly constitute a 'charge', the position is still open and it is highly likely that it will be held not to constitute a charge [7.01 *et seq*] and certainly not a registrable charge [8.01 *et seq*].

Chapter 6

The Prospective Purchaser as Bailee

6.01　What is bailment?

'Bailment is one of the commonest transactions of everyday life' is how N.E. Palmer begins his book, *Bailment*. Common it is, but uncomplicated it is not. Mr Palmer's book on the subject runs to 1054 pages, and contains reference to some 2112 leading cases.

According to Blackstone in his *Commentaries*, written in the 18th Century, the word is derived from the word *bailer*, Norman French for the verb 'to deliver'. It is the obligations imposed by operation of law upon a person, the 'bailee', who is in possession of goods that belong to another.

The classic definition of bailment was that of the present writer's great-uncle Sir Frederick Pollock, who with his co-author, Wright, in their *Possession in the Common Law*, published in 1888, defined a bailee as:

> 'Any person... who otherwise than as a servant, either receives possession of a thing from another or consents to receive or hold possession of a thing from another upon an understanding with the other person either to keep and return or deliver to him the specific thing or to convey and *apply the specific thing according to the directions antecedent or future of the other person.*

This definition was accepted by Winfield in 1932 and by Paton in his *Bailment in the Common Law* in 1952. It is, however, for reasons which are outside the scope of this book, now less than a comprehensive definition.

Apart from wrongful bailment, such as theft of goods, this situation can come about in three major ways:

(a) *Voluntary bailments*, with the consent of both parties. This can be further subdivided into:
   (i) bailment for reward;
   (ii) gratuitous bailment;

(iii) bailments for the benefit of the bailee, as where a person requests the loan of a book or where the parties enter into a contract containing a retention clause;

(iv) bailment for the benefit of the bailor, as where the bailee undertakes gratuitously to look after a cat whilst the owner is away or, where, for reward, he enters into a contract to do the same.

(b) *Involuntary bailment.* In the Australian case of *McCowan* v. *McCulloch* (1926) the defendant mistakenly removed the wrong suitcase from the luggage rack of a train. He made inadequate steps to return it to its owner and because of his negligence it was later stolen. He was held liable as a bailee for the loss.

(c) *Unconscious bailment.* In *AVX Ltd* v. *EGM Solders Ltd* (1982), by mistake 21 boxes of newly finished capacitors were delivered to the defendants along with one box of defective solder spheres. The defendants' servants were ordered to destroy the lot and the capacitors were tipped into skips, mixing 33 different sorts and making them very difficult to sort, before the mistake was discovered. The defendants were held liable, as bailees of the plaintiffs' goods.

6.02   The English law of bailment

Some 18th and 19th Century authors, such as Blackstone and Jones in the United Kingdom, and Story in the United States, seem to consider that all bailments rested on a contract, express or implied.

However, what they ignored was that in early English law, the action *detinue sur bailment* existed alongside the other action of *devenerunt ad manus*, in which the owner of the goods alleged no contract but asserted that his goods were in the possession of the defendant (*devenit ad manus*) – 'they came into his hands'. This was some centuries before the action on the case, *assumpsit*, emerged.

In 1312, in *Lyndesey* v. *Smith* the plaintiff was allowed, subject to establishing the facts, repossession of a charter even though the defendant's counsel raised the defence that there had been no consensual delivery of it. So too, it was claimed in 1344 in *Thornhill's* case that mere possession of another man's property would support an action for detinue: 'In whatever way it came into your possession, if you detain it, I shall have an action'.

Glanville says that if a borrowed thing is lost or destroyed in any way whatsoever there is a strict obligation on the borrower to compensate the owner for its value. Bracton adopts Roman law regarding the contracts of *commodatum*, *depositum* and *pignus* and imposes a like obligation of care on the bailee, but limits the standard of care to *diligentissimus paterfamilias* –

that of the 'utmost diligent father of a family'. He clearly indicates in terms that the obligations of a bailee arise from possession of the goods of another – not from agreement or consent.

In both Crokes' report of *Southcote* v. *Bennett* (1601) and in Coke's report of the same case, it is clear that the obligations of a bailee were founded on possession of the goods alone, and not on any promise or other contractual obligation.

This also appears to have been the view taken by Chief Justice Coke in *Isaack* v. *Clarke* (1615) about involuntary bailees.

> '... for which he findes goods ... if he deliver them over to any one, unless it be unto the right owner, he shall be charged for them, for at the first it is in his election, whether he will take them or not into his custody, but when he hath them, one onely hath the right unto them and therefore he ought to keep them safely.'

This view was also adopted in *Heugh* v. *London & North Western Railway Co.* (1870), where a railway company became the involuntary bailees of various consignments of goods.

American law appears to be the same, since in *Foulke* v. *New York Consolidated R.R.* (1920) it was held that the railway company became the bailee of goods left in a compartment. It was said:

> 'Bailment does not necessarily and always, though generally, depend upon a contractual relation. It is the element of lawful possession, however created, and duty to account for the thing as the property of another that creates the bailment, regardless of whether such possession is based upon contract in the ordinary sense or not.'

This appears to have been recognised in an article by Professor Davidge which appeared in *The Law Quarterly Review* in 1925 which, while it contained many historical errors and an entirely erroneous description of what was decided in the leading case of *Coggs* v. *Bernard* (1703), correctly says:

> 'The bailor does not sue the defaulting bailee for breach of contract; the bailee in refusing to return, or in damaging the bailor's goods is guilty of a tort and in common with all other torts in early days liability in bailment was absolute.
>
> It was no excuse for the bailee to say that the damage or the failure to return was due to no fault of his own; he was liable in any case.'

For this reason, Alice Erk Soon Tay in *The Essence of a Bailment* in *The Sydney Law Review*, it is submitted, correctly says:

'The primary duty of a man who takes into his possession the chattel of another without challenging the other's title is the same whether he be a hirer, a borrower, a finder or an involuntary bailee.'

It can therefore be confidently asserted that the conception of bailment rests on possession of the goods of another and not on the existence of any contractual relationship.

As Fifoot said in his *History and Sources of the Common Law*:

'Bailment is in truth *sui generis* – an elementary and unique transaction, the practical necessity of which is self-evident and self-explanatory and if in later years it is most often, though not invariably, associated with a contract, this is not and never has been its essential characteristic. It was a familiar fact, as Detinue and Debt were familiar words long before contract was conceived.'

6.03   Do the goods bailed have to be returned to the bailor?

The proposition that there can only be a bailment when the very goods themselves have to be returned to the bailor, as advanced by Mr Justice Slade in *In re Bond Worth Ltd* [1.05] is not supported by Roman or English law.

As has been seen from Pollock and Wright's definition [6.01], the obligation of the bailee is to return the goods bailed to the bailor *or to dispose of them in accordance with the directions of the bailor*. Hence, in later Roman law and in English law for at least the last three centuries there could be a bailment where the bailor never intended to repossess the goods but intended to allow them, in due course, to become the property of the bailee. The common kinds are, of course, hire purchase and conditional sales [5.01]. But an auctioneer was long ago held to be a bailee: *R* v. *Prince* (1827). There was no question there of the goods having to be returned intact to the bailor.

None of the cases advanced by Mr Justice Slade support his proposition.

In *In ex parte White* (1873) cotton goods were sent by Towle & Co. to one Nevill on terms that he sold them on such terms as he pleased and did not pay for them until he had in fact disposed of them. The question whether Nevill was in a fiduciary relationship with Towle, or whether it was a simple creditor/debtor relationship, was disposed of by Lord Justice James with the words:

'It does not appear that he was ever expected to return any particular contract, or the names of the persons with whom he had dealt.

He pursued his own course in dealing with the goods, and frequently before sale he manipulated them to a very considerable extent by pressing, dyeing and otherwise altering their character, changing them as much as wheat would be changed by being turned into flour; and he sold them on what terms he pleased as to price and length of credit.

No question appears ever to have been raised as to whether he was entitled to do this; we must take it that he did not commit any breach of duty in so doing.

That is quite inconsistent with the notion that he was acting in a fiduciary character in respect of those goods.

If he was entitled to alter them, to manipulate them, to sell them at any price that he thought fit after they had been so manipulated, and was still only liable to pay for them at a price fixed beforehand, without any reference to the price at which he had sold them, or to anything else than the fact of his having sold them in a certain month, it seems to me impossible to say that the produce of the goods so sold was the money of the consignors or that the relation of vendor and purchaser existed between Towle & Co. and the different persons to whom he sold the goods.'

Mr Justice Slade apparently saw some analogy between the facts in that case and those in *Romalpa*. But in the *ex parte White* case, property in the goods clearly passed to Nevill on delivery and the only difference from the usual agreement to sell was the terms on which he was allowed to pay for them. It would not appear to be relevant to a situation where title was expressly retained in the vendor; in this case the buyer was not a bailee for the simple reason that he was the owner. What he did with the goods was only of evidential value as to whether title had passed to him or not.

The House of Lords' case of *Foley* v. *Hill* (1848) was the one in which it was held that the relationship between banker and customer was that between debtor and creditor. Money is not, by definition of the Sale of Goods Act 1893 or 1979 'goods'; although bailment may apply to coins or notes in which the property would normally pass on delivery. The reason is that recipients of money are not normally required to return the identical coins or notes to the bailors. Their duty is simply to return the same sum. However, there can be circumstances in which the recipient of coins or notes can be held to be a bailee and not a debtor; *Walker* v. *British Guarantee Association* (1852); *Thomas* v. *High* (1960); *R* v. *Geake* (1896).

That there can be a bailment of money is evident from *Moukataff* v. *B.O.A.C.* (1967) where the plaintiff ordered his London bank to send by post £20,000 in bank notes to a bank in Kuwait. The Post Office received the notes and arranged with B.O.A.C., as it then was, to carry the notes to Kuwait. While loading, one of the airline's servants stole the notes. The airline were held liable as bailees. Here, once again, the goods – the sterling notes – were never to be returned to the bailor: the obligation was to carry them to be paid into a bank in Kuwait.

The case of *Foley* v. *Hill* (1848) is therefore certainly not authority for the proposition that there can never be a bailment unless the goods originally bailed have themselves to be returned to the bailor.

South Australian Insurance Co. v. *Randell* (1869) turned on whether a miller who received farmers' corn for grinding but was under no obligation to return the very same corn but an equivalent quantity had an insurable interest in the corn.

It is difficult to see what assistance any of these cases would have been to the Court of Appeal in its task of construing clause 13 of the *Romalpa* agreement, as Mr Justice Slade suggested. Clearly, there can be a bailment even though the goods bailed never are intended ever to return to the bailee. Even in the leading case of *Coggs* v. *Barnard* (or Bernard) (1703), the brandy was on the way to the cellars of Gray's Inn and would never have returned to the bailor – unless he had drunk water from the Thames.

6.04   Can there be a bailment where the bailee is entitled to process the goods bailed?

Another of the erroneous propositions of law advanced by Mr Justice Slade in *In re Bond Worth Ltd*, was one that there could be no relationship of bailor and bailee if the bailee was authorised to process and/or incorporate the goods bailed into other products. In fact his lordship expressly approved the argument advanced by counsel that

> 'It is quite inconsistent with the concept of a trust or fiduciary relationship ... that Bond Worth should be free to use the Acrilan fibre and other categories of assets subject to the retention of title clause for the purpose of its own business and manufacturing processes.'

This involves two propositions: there can be no bailment where the goods are to be subjected to a process which will fundamentally change their nature; and there can be no bailment where the goods are to be incorporated with other goods.

The second proposition is discussed in detail in the next chapter in relation to the Admixture of Goods [7.01 et seq.]. But the obvious falsity of this contention can be seen in a simple proposition. Suppose I send my car into a garage for a new engine. The garage man is then undoubtedly the bailee of my car. He puts a new engine, his property, into my car. Does he thereby cease to be the bailee of my car? Of course not. All he gets is the right to be paid for his goods and a lien over my car for his work and materials until he is. That is: a mere right to detain my property. In no way does he cease to be bailee of my car. If he were to sell it to somebody else or failed to take proper care of it, he would – undoubtedly – be liable to me as a bailee.

The first proposition in itself scarcely merits more discussion. Since Roman times, it has been recognised that there is a bailment whenever a person is entrusted with goods to work on them, either for reward or gratuitously. *Mandatum* was the term where the work was to be done without remuneration: *Locatio operis faciendi* where goods were entrusted to a person to process them for reward. The goods remained in the bailee's possession until the work was done when they, in their new form, were to be returned to the bailor, or otherwise dealt with in accordance with his directions.

There are dozens of everyday examples of *locatio operis faciendi*, which Chief Justice Holt in the leading case of *Coggs* v. *Barnard* (or Bernard) in 1703 defined as:

'when goods or chattels are delivered ... [for] something to be done about them for a reward to be paid by the person who delivers them to the bailee who is to do something about them.'

Common examples of these in everyday life are sheets sent to a laundry, or clothes entrusted to a dry cleaners.

There can be such bailments when the goods are to be substantially changed by the process. Examples include leather into shoes (*Mansfield* v. *Converse*) and milk into cheese (*Bank* v. *Schween*). These cases were quoted in *D.M. Ferry & Co.* v. *Forquer* (1921) where it was said:

'In these cases, the transaction is a bailment and it is altogether immaterial whether the compensation of the bailee is fixed at a definite sum in money or is a share of the product itself, a share of the net proceeds, a share of the increase, or is computed upon the product of the undertaking.'

In that particular case it was held that there was a bailment of seed where the seed was entrusted to a farmer to be planted and raised on his land and that the bailment extended to what was grown from the seed. This is now a common transaction. The frozen goods manufacturers develop their own species of peas. They do not sell them to farmers but entrust them to them for reward, calculated on yield. The farmer is bailee of the seed and of the produce of it. They are not at liberty to dispose of the crop otherwise than yielding it up to the bailors or disposing of it in accordance with their directions.

It is therefore undoubtedly established law that there can be bailment not only when the bailee alters the goods to a minor extent but where he totally transforms them into what are substantially different goods. With grapes there is a bailment of the grapes until they are pressed; there is a bailment of the juice while it is fermenting; there is a bailment of the skins of the grapes; and there is a bailment of the final product, the fermented wine.

There is, therefore, no reason whatsoever why there should not be bailment of goods which are totally transformed by a process.

What happens to them after they have been processed is a matter entirely for the owner. If he cares to license the processor and prospective purchaser to sell them on his own behalf and as an agent for the owner, there is no reason whatsoever why that should not be done.

6.05   The consequence of a bailment

If the prospective purchaser is the bailee of the goods, there are obligations imposed upon him both by the common law and by equity. As Lord Jessel MR said in *In re Hallett's Estate* (1880):

> 'The modern doctrine of equity as regards property disposed of by persons in a fiduciary position is a very clear and well established doctrine.
>
> You can ... take the proceeds of sale if you can identify them.
>
> If a bailee sells the goods bailed the bailor can in equity follow the proceeds ... therefore there is no difficulty – in following the rule of equity and deciding that in the case of a mere bailee ... you can follow the money.'

As Mr Justice Mocatta said in the *Romalpa* case:

> 'It is not necessary to find as a prerequisite of the right to trace an express or constructive trust.'

The equitable proprietary remedy follows as a consequence of the finding that the defendants were bailees.

As Professor Pennington said about the *Romalpa* case [5.03]:

'The contract made mention of the possibility of resale, and this was sufficient to put the defendant in a position where it was a fiduciary of the proceeds of resale. Thus, if a contract of sale envisages the resale of the goods by the buyer, then when the buyer resells he is made an agent for the seller by the terms of the contract and he has a fiduciary obligation to account for the proceeds of resale to the seller.'

6.06 The right to trace proceeds at common law

This right to trace arises at common law as well as in equity, so that it can exist even where there is no fiduciary relationship.

In *Taylor* v. *Plumer* (1815), the defendant owned government stock. He handed his stock certificates to a stockbroker with instructions to sell and re-invest the proceeds in other stock. The stockbroker duly sold his stock but invested the proceeds in American Government bearer bonds, and was arrested as he was about to leave for the United States. The plaintiff was the stockbroker's trustee in bankruptcy who had sold the bearer bonds for the benefit of the stockbroker's bankrupt estate and claimed to be entitled to retain the proceeds. He claimed that Plumer had only a right to damages for breach of contract and no title to the American Government bonds.

The court accepted the proposition that where there is wrongful taking of property, it is possible at common law to trace the proceeds into the monies received and thence into whatever assets the monies have acquired. Plumer was entitled to the American Government bearer bonds and the proceeds of their sale. He was, at common law, entitled to trace the government stocks which were his property into the proceeds of sale, and thence into the American Government bearer bonds and thence into the proceeds in money received for those by the trustee. He was not restricted to a claim for damages, which would have relegated him to the position of an unsecured creditor, with no hope of reimbursement.

This case is highly relevant to the situation where a receiver sells goods subject to a retention of title clause. He is selling somebody else's property, which is the tort of conversion and is therefore a wrongful act. If, therefore, the sub-purchaser has yet to pay the receiver, it may well be that the original seller can, at common law, insist that the payment be made in full to him.

However, it seems possible that this common law tracing right may be lost if the proceeds of sale were admixed with other monies, so that they could not be separately identified.

The common law rights are therefore limited, but if a company, for example, acquired machinery subject to a retention of title clause for its own use, but it or a receiver sold the machinery, there clearly would have been a conversion of the sellers' goods. The proceeds would therefore be the sellers' property and they would not be in the usual unhappy position of an unsecured creditor. If payment had not been made by the sub-purchaser, the sellers could require the purchase price to be paid direct to themselves; and they are entitled by an *ex parte* injunction to restrain the receiver from mingling the proceeds with other monies and require that it should be deposited in a separate, identifiable, bank account.

6.07   The fiduciary obligations of a bailee

Each and every bailee is under an obligation to account to the bailor for the proceeds of sale of the goods bailed. It matters not whether the sale is lawful or unlawful.

As Lord Jessel MR said in the *In re Hallett case*

'Now that being the established doctrine of equity on this point, I will take the case of the pure bailee. If the bailee sells the goods bailed, the bailor can in equity follow the proceeds ... Therefore there is no difficulty in following the rule of equity and deciding that in a case of mere bailee ... you can follow the money.'

He also made it plain that there was no difference between a bailee who is by law in a fiduciary position and trustees constituted under an express trust. He said:

'Has it ever been suggested, until very recently, that there was any distinction between an express trustee, or an agent, or a bailee, or a collector of rents or anybody else in a fiduciary position? I have never heard, until quite recently, such a distinction suggested ... It can have no foundation in principle, because the beneficial ownership is the same, wherever the legal ownership may be.'

In *In re Hallett's Estate* a solicitor had misappropriated trust money and had wrongfully invested it, partly in his own name, mixing some of the trust's money with his own. Lord Jessel MR commented in his judgment:

'Where a trustee has mixed the money with his own there is this distinction that the beneficial owner can no longer elect to take the property because it is no longer bought with the trust money simply and purely but with a mixed fund. He is however still entitled to a charge on the property purchased ...'

... the moment you establish the fiduciary relation the modern rules of equity as regards following trust monies apply ...

According to law, the bankers are his debtors for the total amount, but if you lend the trust money to a third person you can follow it ...

Supposing the trustee had lent £1000 to a man without security you could follow the debt and take it from the debtor.'

The Master of the Rolls, in this case, which established the right to trace, made it clear that the principles on which his judgment were based were of a general nature and could be applied with equal merit in the field of commercial law.

6.08   Can there be a bailee without fiduciary obligations?

Mr Justice Staughton in *Hendy Lennox (Industrial Engines) Ltd* v. *Grahame Puttick Ltd* (1984) apparently expressed the opinion that there could be a bailment without any fiduciary obligation to the bailor. He said:

'Notwithstanding an earlier passage in the judgment of Roskill LJ which might suggest otherwise it is, I think, implicit in the reasoning in the Court of Appeal in the *Romalpa* case that some bailees and some agents do not occupy a fiduciary position, although there may well be a presumption that they do.'

His lordship did not indicate how or why the Court of Appeal had reached such an extraordinary conclusion or where it is to be found in the *Romalpa* case. With respect it is neither implicit, still less explicit.

However, since he concluded that it was unnecessary for him to hold whether the buyers were or were not bailees, his observations must be regarded as entirely *obiter dicta*, and inconsistent with earlier centuries of accepted law.

6.09   Tracing into other goods

It is quite apparent therefore that if a bailee sells goods, with or without the consent of the bailor, both the common law and equity will attach the owner's rights to the monetary proceeds of sale. Further, the owner can trace these proceeds into any property acquired by the monetary proceeds, whether it be American bearer bonds, real estate or a motor car or any other goods.

As Lord Jessel said so clearly:

> 'If the bailee sells the goods bailed the bailor can in equity follow the proceeds ... wherever they can be distinguished.'

It is not surprising, therefore, that Judge Rubin QC sitting as a deputy judge of the Chancery Division of the High Court, held that by operation of law where goods subject to a retention of title clause were incorporated with those of the bailee, the bailor could trace his goods into the finished product and the proceeds thereof: *Borden (UK) Ltd* v. *Scottish Timber Products Ltd* (1979).

Borden (UK) Ltd supplied resin to Scottish Timber Products Ltd between 14 February and 16 September 1977, when a receiver was appointed. The resin was delivered by road tanker and stored in tanks which, if full to capacity, held only enough resin to keep the S.T.P. factory working for two days.

When required for use, the resin was transferred to a separate tank where it was mixed with wax emulsion and hardeners to form a glue mix. It was then blended with dessicated timber and pressed to form chipboard. Of the final chipboard, the timber components comprised 24% by value and the resin 17%.

The retention of title clause read:

Clause 2: Risk and property
Goods supplied by the company shall be at the purchaser's risk immediately on delivery to the purchaser or into custody on the purchaser's behalf (whichever is the sooner) and the purchaser should therefore be insured accordingly. Property on the goods supplied hereunder will pass to the customer when (a) the goods the subject of the contract (b) all other goods the subject any other contract between the company and the customer which at the time of payment of the full price of the goods sold under the contract, have been delivered to the customer, but not paid in full, have been paid for in full.

It will be seen that it was, so far as (a) is concerned, a simple retention clause, and so far as (b) is concerned, a current account clause, not for all indebtedness but limited to indebtedness for previous deliveries of goods. There was, however, no aggregation clause.

Judge Rubin held that the following were the issues:

(1) Did Borden have any proprietary interest at common law in any chipboard manufactured by S.T.P. using the resin supplied by Borden?
(2) What right, if any, has Borden on the principle of *In re Hallett* to trace their resin into its proceeds of sale?
(3) Whether any such right to trace was a charge which was void by reason of section 95 of the Companies Act 1948, against creditors of the company?

On the second point, he said:

'It seemed to me clear from an early stage in the argument that S.T.P. received resin which remained the property of Borden as a bailee for Borden, and accordingly a fiduciary relationship was created.

If instead of using that resin for manufacture S.T.P. had resold part of it ... on the principle of *In re Hallett's Estate*, Borden would have been able to trace its resin into the proceeds of any such sale.

That was precisely the conclusion which was reached by the Court of Appeal in *Aluminium Industrie Vaassen B.V.* v. *Romalpa Aluminium Ltd* ...

In the present case, there is no reason even to imply a power to sell resin as resin, let alone a power for S.T.P. to sell it for its own account.

In the end the defendants' counsel accepted, though with reluctance, that Borden would be entitled to trace into the proceeds of sale any sale of resin as resin.

The defendants argued that the tracing remedy does not extend where there is a use in manufacture to the manufactured product and its proceeds of sale.

In my judgment, unless the fiduciary relationship was brought to an end by the use in manufacture, or it is possible to imply a further term into the contract that S.T.P. would be entitled to deal with the chipboard on its own account, there is no reason why the tracing remedy should not extend both to the chipboard and its proceeds of sale.

Counsel for the defendants argued both strongly and repeatedly that I should imply no terms at all into the contract or if I implied a licence to use the resin in manufacture I should imply no further term.

This appears to be an argument against his interest, but I agree that there is no scope in the present case for implying any term beyond a bare licence to use in manufacture before payment.

In *In re Hallett's Estate*, Lord Jessel MR after considering the nature of the equitable remedy said:

"Therefore the moment you establish the fiduciary relationship, the modern rules of equity, as regards following trust money apply."

and in the last paragraph on that page he said:

"Now, that being the established doctrine of equity on the point, I will take the case of the pure bailee. If the bailee sells the goods bailed, the bailor can in equity follow the proceeds, and can follow the proceeds wherever they can be distinguished, either being actually kept separate, or being mixed up with other moneys."

The Master of the Rolls then used an example of a bailee holding a sum of sovereigns which he mixed with his own sovereigns and then invested in a bond or promissory note and said that the only difference was that instead of taking the bond or promissory note, the *cestui que trust* would have a charge for the amount of the trust money on the bond or promissory note.

If instead of sovereigns, the bailee has some other physical article in his possession which he mixes with his own property in such a way that the trust property could no longer be identified and separated, then, in my view, by like reasoning the *cestui que trust* would have a charge for the value of his property over the mass of the combined property or its proceeds of sale.

I was referred to *Kirkham* v. *Peel* (1881) as a case which limited the principles of *Hallett's* case. In my judgment that case does no such thing. It merely establishes upon the true construction of the express terms of that contract, assisted by terms to be implied, that the defendants were bound to account for the balance of the proceeds of sale and as they had done this, no question of tracing arose. It is no authority for the proposition that if they had failed to account, the plaintiff would not have been entitled to have a charge upon any asset of the defendants into which he could have traced the proceeds of sale.'

Judge Rubin then discussed the *Romalpa* case and concluded:

'Once it is accepted that initially S.T.P. received resin as a bailee and accordingly that a fiduciary relationship arose, then, in my judgment, the tracing remedies must be available to Borden unless it can be shown that one ought to imply into the contract a power to use the resin in manufacture and if so a liberty in S.T.P. to hold any goods so manufactured to its own account.

I have already decided that in particular by reason of the limited storage capacity I can imply a licence to use in manufacture but I can see no valid reason why I should imply any further term.

Indeed S.T.P.'s counsel urged me very strongly not to imply any terms at all.'

The judge, with impeccable logic, it is submitted, therefore concluded

'that Borden was entitled to trace any of its resin supplied after 14 February 1977, the title to which had not passed to S.T.P. under clause 2 of the contract, into any chipboard manufactured from such resin or into the proceeds of sale of such chipboard, but so that Borden could not recover a sum in excess of the contract price of such resin.'

However, the Court of Appeal overruled that judgment for reasons which are discussed in detail in the next chapter but which in substance were based on an incredible concession by counsel for Borden that ownership in the resin disappeared when it was incorporated with other material.

Chapter 7

English Law Regarding Admixture of Goods

7.01 'Title simply disappeared'?

In the Court of Appeal in *Borden* v. *Scottish Timber Products Ltd* [6.09] counsel for Borden made a concession which, as will be seen, was wrong in law and fatal to his case. Lord Justice Bridge described it thus:

> 'I am quite content to assume . . . that up to the moment when resin was used in manufacture, it was held by S.T.P. in trust for Borden in the same sense in which a bailee or a factor or an agent holds goods in trust for his bailor or his principal.
>
> If that was the position, then there is no doubt that as soon as the resin was used in the manufacturing process it ceased to exist as resin and *accordingly the title to the resin simply disappeared.*
>
> So much is accepted [by counsel] for the respondent, Borden.'

With respect, it must be said that chattels do not simply disappear because they are admixed with other chattels; nor is the title to them extinguished by admixture with other goods. As Mr Justice Blackburn said in *Buckley* v. *Gross* (1863):

> 'Probably the legal effects of such a mixture would be to make the owners tenants in common in equal portions of the mass, *but at all events they do not lose their property in it.*'

English law has few cases, by contrast with Roman law, on the effect of admixture. All of them deal with accidental admixture. What cases there are do not in any way support the proposition that the identity of chattels admixed with other chattels 'simply disappears': *Spence* v. *Union Marine* (1868); *Sinclair* v. *Brougham* (1914); (see also Holdsworth: *History of English Law*, Volume VII, page 502).

7.02 Roman law of aggregation

A useful starting point to consider this question is Roman Law. Unlike most of the legal systems of continental Europe and Scotland, the English common law is not based on Roman law. However, it is always helpful to look at Roman law initially.

The Romans were very good at analysing situations and legal problems so that their questions are invariably of value even if their answers are not the ones that the common law would give. Moreover, where there are lacunae in English law, the courts adopt Roman Law. Strangely enough, in all the many thousands of decisions in the English courts, there was no law about who owned a swarm of bees. The courts therefore followed Roman Law.

The Romans distinguished between three separate situations: *accessio*, *confusio* and *commixtio* (Justinian, Lib. II, Tit. 1; Digest 6.1.23.5). *Accessio* was the situation where something trifling in value was added to a more substantial article: for example, writing in ink was added to a parchment. *Confusio* dealt with the position where goods were so combined as to be later inseparable: the admixture of two liquids, or where A's purple was used for dyeing B's garment. The third situation, *commixtio*, was where there was the admixture of the chattels of two owners in such a way that they could readily be separated.

In modern times, where A's paint is used to paint B's motor car we have *accessio*. A's resin is mixed with B's dessicated wood: *confusio*. An engine or new tyres are put by B on A's motor car: *commixtio*.

7.03 English law about *commixtio*

It is proposed to treat this subject first, since the law is comparatively simple.

A passage in Halsbury's *Laws of England*, 2nd Edition, Volume 25, page 208, (in substance repeated in different words in the 3rd Edition, Volume 29, page 378) advanced the proposition that the law regarding the admixture of chattels to other chattels replicates the law about the fixtures and land. It read:

'If any corporeal substance receives an accession by natural or artificial means as by the growth of vegetables, the pregnancy of animals, the embroidery of cloth, or the conversion of wood or metal into vessels or utensils, the original owner is entitled by his right of possession to the property in its improved state.

Similarly when the goods of one man are affixed to the land or chattel, for example, a ship of another, they may become part of it and so accrue to the owner of the particular thing.'

The passage is undoubtedly correct in so far as land is concerned [3.05]. But, as Professor Sawyer pointed out as long ago as 1935 in *The Australian Law Journal*, Volume 9, page 50:

'The rule of law identifying things attached to land with the land itself is an independent rule springing from the peculiar importance of land in English legal history as compared with personal property and this rule has never been thought to apply in any way to chattels.

'The earliest actions arose on actions of waste, applicable only to land and the discussions in the classic books and the many cases cited by them ... are concerned only with land.'

He also pointed out that the maxim *quicquid plantatur solo, solo cedit* ('whatever is attached to the soil becomes part of the soil') is exclusively English law and that Roman Law was 'substantially different', quoting Buckland's *Textbook of Roman Law*, page 214 ff, and Sohm's *Institutes*, page 326 ff. Professor Sawyer then examined three cases which, it was sometimes claimed, supported the proposition in Halsbury and concluded that none of them did in fact do so. The three cases are *Forman* v. *The Liddlesdale* (1900); *Appleby* v. *Myers* (1867) and *Sinclair & Ano.* v. *Bowles* (1829) (which would have succeeded had it been framed in detinue).

He concluded that if the joinder of two chattels is not of such a durable nature, so that 'the chattels can be easily severed without damage to either, no change of ownership takes place at all'. In this, English law is, he suggested, the same as Roman law: *Buckland* page 210, Manual 139 ff; *Blackstone*, Volume II, Chapters XXVI, 6 and 7.

Few legal articles can have been more influential than this one by Professor Sawyer. His propositions have been adopted through the common law world. To take but one example: in *Lewis* v. *Andrews & Rowley Property Company Ltd* (1956), what was described as 'a trailer' was leased on weekly terms and subject to a term that 'all spare parts and accessories supplied and fitted to the vehicle' should remain the property of the lessee. The vehicle was seized by a mortgagee and on her behalf it was argued that all the parts, including tyres, fitted to the vehicle had become her property. 'The submission was ... that irrespective of any intention to transfer the property and irrespective of detachability, if an article is attached to the chattel of another so as to become incorporated with it, that article ceases to have an independent existence and becomes part of the chattel,' said Chief Justice Roper. The New South Wales Supreme Court held that irrespective of the contractual terms, the property in the tyres and other accessories and parts fitted remained the property of the lessee:

> 'If A's goods can be separated from B's no problem arises and each is entitled to his own.'

The problem frequently arises in connection with leased aircraft which have replacement engines fitted and with hire purchase vehicles where the hirer incorporates his own items, such as tyres or wing mirrors.

Although there are few cases in the English books about such situations, there are dozens in other common law countries such as the United States, Australia and Canada. A typical one is the case in the Canadian Supreme Court, *Firestone Tyre & Rubber Co.* v. *Industrial Acceptance Corporation* (1971) where a man took possession of a truck under a conditional sale agreement and put new tyres on it, which were also acquired under a conditional sale agreement. The truck was repossessed and the owners claimed to be entitled to the tyres. It was held that the tyres, being removable and identifiable accessory chattels still belonged to those who had supplied them. Laskin J said:

> 'There is no justification ... in this case for giving the respondent a windfall against a third party who has reserved title.'

It is therefore usual for hire purchase agreements to include express terms that all accessories or replacement goods fitted shall become the property of the hirer. (See A.G. Guest, *Accession and Confusion in the Law of Hire Purchase*, 27 Modern Law Review pp 505–520; A.G. Guest and J. Lever, *Hire Purchase Equipment Leases and Fixtures*, 27 Conveyancer pp 30–44; J.L.C. Wickham, *The Struggle for Title*, 5 University of Western Australian L.R. pp 496–497; *Protection of Chattel Mortgagees*, 41 Iowa Law Review pp 628–640.)

Such clauses may be effective where the hirer puts his own property, such as tyres on to the vehicle, but it seems clear that such clauses cannot prevail against a third party whose property is added to the vehicle, since he is not a party to the conditional sale or hire purchase agreement: see R.D. Nicholson *Accessory Clauses in Motor Vehicle Hire Purchase Agreements* 39 A.L.J. 408.

All these cases, however, make it quite clear that the contracting parties are at liberty to make whatever provision they like about the ownership of commixted goods.

7.04 Retention of title and identifiable goods

These principles seemed to have been applied in *Hendy Lennox (Industrial Engines) Ltd* v. *Grahame Puttick Ltd* (1983). The plaintiffs were main dealers for the Ford Motor Company and supplied diesel engines and spare parts to the defendants for incorporation into diesel generating sets.

In his judgment Mr Justice Staughton said:

'The process of incorporation would not in any way alter or destroy the substance of the engine. It would remain identified by the serial number which the sellers or the Ford motor company had given it; it would be attached by bolts to the generator and by various other connections to items such as a fuel tank (and a radiator for coolant. I should add that the radiator is apparently not part of the engine.) But the engine would not physically be changed; the connections could be undone and the engine removed within a period described in the evidence as "several hours." I was told that this vague expression was used by agreement so that it would be unnecessary to resolve a minor dispute between the parties as to the actual period of time required.'

The engines were sold on a retention of title clause which included the terms:

'10. Payment. (i) The terms of payment specified overleaf or as stated on the official quotation and/or acknowledgement of order shall apply and if none be specified then payment in full shall be made at the time when the goods are ready for delivery. Unless the company shall otherwise specify in writing *all goods sold by the company to the purchaser shall be and remain the property of the company until the full purchase price thereof shall be paid to the company*. In the case of default in payment by the purchaser, the company shall have the right to retake possession of and permanently retain any unpaid for goods and to revoke all liability of the company to the purchaser on the contract of sale and delivery of such goods ...

12. Termination. The company shall have the right immediately to terminate the contract at any time upon occurrence of any of the following events:

(i) if the purchaser commits any act of bankruptcy or compounds or makes any arrangements with his creditors or executes a bill of sale on his goods or any of them or if any execution or distress is levied upon the goods of the purchaser.

(ii) If the purchaser being a company is wound up either compulsorily or voluntarily or a receiver of its assets is appointed.

(iii) If the purchaser fails to take delivery of any of the goods subject to the contract.

Upon any such termination of the contract the company shall have the right either:

(a) to require the purchaser to take over and pay for at the then current price such materials as the company shall have allocated to the contract including labour and other expense incurred by the company in relation to such materials, or
(b) to dispose of the said materials at its discretion without being liable to account to the purchaser for the proceeds of such disposal.'

Mr Justice Staughton concluded:

'I am aware that until very recently the radio and radar apparatus on a ship was commonly hired by the shipowner rather than bought by him. No doubt it was attached to the ship: but I do not suppose that it thereby became the property of the shipowner or his mortgagee. Nor in my judgment would an engine which was the property of A become the property of B merely because B incorporated it in a generator set otherwise composed of his own materials.

Those reflections and the facts of this case persuade me that the proprietary rights of the sellers in the engines were not affected when the engines were wholly or partially incorporated into generator sets.'

In that, he specifically rejected the passage set out in Halsbury's *Laws of England*, Third Edition, Volume 29, page 378, [7.03] which had been quoted to him.

7.05 Indissoluble aggregation of chattels in English law

More difficult problems arise where there is *accessio* in the Roman sense – the accretion of minor parts to a major chattel – and *confusio*, the indissoluble union of diverse chattels to form a new whole.

It is submitted that two paramount principles apply. The first principle is that the provisions regarding transfer of title made by the Sale of Goods Act 1979, are binding on all parties to a transaction subject to the Act. The second is that, subject to the statute, the parties are free to make such contractual arrangements as to the passing of title as they choose.

Section 17 of the Sale of Goods Act provides:

'(1) Where there is a contract for the sale of specific or ascertained goods the property in them is transferred to the buyer at such time as the parties to the contract intend it to be transferred.

(2) For the purpose of ascertaining the intention of the parties regard shall be had to the terms of the contract, the conduct of the parties and the circumstances of the case.'

Chief Justice Roper was less than strictly accurate when he said in *Lewis* v. *Andrews & Rowley Pty. Ltd* (1956) that it

'is a general rule of English law that property in chattels is transferred only when the owner so intends.'

But, in effect, that is the position; the seller can determine when the property shall pass to the intending buyer. Diamonds were sent to an intending purchaser by post with a bill of exchange drawn on him and an invoice marked 'settled by acceptance'. When the intending purchaser did not accept the bill of exchange it was held that the ownership remained with the seller: *Saks* v. *Tilley* (1915).

Apart from specific contractual obligations, where goods are admixed in circumstances where there is no tort, the position appears to be that there is a choice between:

(1) 'The title in the goods simply disappears' – per Lord Justice Bridge in the *Borden* case, based on a concession by counsel for Borden.
(2) The owner of the more substantial chattel becomes the owner of the whole – subject to an equitable obligation to compensate the other owner, or if done without consent, to pay damages for conversion.
(3) The two owners become in law joint owners as tenants in common in shares appropriate to their contribution in value to the finished product.

It can be said at once that there is no authority whatsoever to support the first proposition; indeed there are a multitude of observations to the effect that if goods are admixed the owners do not lose their property in them.

The authority in English courts for either of the two other propositions is meagre.

There is a wealth of early authority about the effect of tortious admixture: Moore 19; Popham 38; Hale P.C. 512; *Lupton* v. *White* (1808); *Jones* v. *Moore* (1841).

The undoubted principle of both common law and equity was that anyone who had undertaken to keep the property of another distinct from his own but who mixed it with his own without authority thereby conferred title in the whole on the other owner. The burden of proof of what share was his rested on him and he could only recover if he could prove what was his share: *Lupton* v. *White* (1808). This was a case about the unlawful extraction of lead ore from a mine by an adjacent mine owner. The then Lord Chancellor said:

> 'What are the cases in the old law of a mixture of corn or flour? If one man mixes his corn or flour with that of another, and they were of equal value, the latter must have the given quantity: but, if articles of different value are mixed, producing a third value, the aggregate of both, and through the fault of the person mixing them, the other party cannot tell, what was the original value of his property, he must have the whole and the principle goes to the full extent of what is now contended. Regretting the consequences in this instance to one of the parties, who is made answerable only for inattention to his own interest, I believe, there is no greater violation of property in this country than of property of this nature.'

He added:

> 'Sir William Blackstone observes the distinction between the civil law and our law upon this point: the former, though giving the aggregate to the party, who did not interfere in the mixture, allowing the other a satisfaction for his loss: "but our law, to guard against fraud, gives the entire property, without any account, to him, whose original dominion is invaded, and endeavoured to be rendered uncertain, without his own consent."'

But there are few cases which deal with the principles with which we are concerned.

Bracton inaccurately reproduced Roman law: see Maitland *Bracton & Azo*, page 113–17. Blackstone also purported to follow Roman Law and mentions an extraordinary case of *accessio* in which a husband recovered his wife (herself treated as a chattel) from her lover, who brought an unsuccessful action for the value of the clothes which she was wearing when she was repossessed. It is not, one would have thought, a very valuable precedent for the twentieth century.

There may be a poverty of English law on the subject, but guidance can be gleaned from earlier English cases on the accidental admixture of materials.

In 1885 the merchant ship *Caroline Nasmyth* sailed from Mobile in the USA with a cargo of cotton bound for Liverpool. She had on board 2493 bales belonging to different owners and shipped under separate bills of lading. The *Caroline Nasmyth* was wrecked on the Florida reef fifty miles from Key West and her cargo was either sold there or transhipped into another vessel bound for Liverpool. When the remainder arrived, the marks were so obliterated by sea-water that they could not be identified.

It was claimed by the plaintiffs that this was a total loss for which they were entitled to be indemnified by their insurers. The court, however, held that this was not so. The plaintiffs became joint owners as tenants in common of all the unidentified cotton bales.

The court specifically relied upon Roman Law and said:

'In our own law there are not many authorities to be found upon this subject; but, as far as they go, they are in favour of the view that, when goods of different owners become by accident so mixed together as to be indistinguishable, the owners of the goods so mixed become tenants in common of the whole, in the proportions which they have severally contributed to it.

The passage cited from the judgment of Blackburn J, in the case of the tallow which was melted and flowed into the sewers, is to that effect: *Buckley* v. *Gross* (1863).

And a similar mixture was adopted by Lord Abinger in the case of the mixture of oil by leakage on board ship, in *Jones* v. *Moore* (1841).

It has been long settled in our law, that, where goods are mixed so as to become indistinguishable by the wrongful act or default of one owner, he cannot recover, and will not be entitled to his proportion, or any part of the property, from the other owner; but no authority has been cited to show that any such principle has ever been applied, nor indeed could it be applied, to the case of an accidental mixing of the goods of two owners; and there is no authority nor sound reason for saying that the goods of several persons which are accidentally mixed together thereby absolutely cease to be the property of their several owners and become *bona vacantia*.

The goods being before they are mixed the separate property of the several owners, unless, which is absurd, they cease to be property by reason of the accidental mixture, when they would not so cease if the mixture were designed, must continue to be the property of the original owners, and as there would be no means of distinguishing the goods of each, the several owners seem necessarily to become jointly interested, as tenants in common, in the bulk.'

This is the rule of the Roman Law as stated in Mackeldey's Modern Civil Law, under the title *Commixtio et Confusio*, in the special part, Book 1, section 270. In the English edition of 1845, at p. 285 the passage is as follows:

"The mixing together of things solid or dry (*commixtio*) or of things liquid (*confusio*) which belong to different owners has no effect upon their rights in the things, if the latter can be separated. If, on the other hand, such separation is not practicable, then the former proprietors of the things now connected will be joint owners of the whole, *whenever the mixture has been made with the consent of both parties*, or by accident."

"We need not discuss the distinction sometimes made between *commixtio* and *confusio*, apparently upon the ground that it is possible to separate the individual solid particles, but not the liquid; because, in cases like the present, it is impracticable, and for all business purposes therefore impossible, to distinguish the particles in respect of ownership.

The passages in Mr Justice Story's work on Bailments, s. 40, and in the 9th volume of Pothier, *De La Confusion*, as well as the French and various other codes are to the same effect."

In *Jones* v. *Moore* (1841) the vessel *Dorothy Gales* was carrying a cargo of oil in different casks for various shippers from Columbo, Ceylon, to London. On the way, several of the casks leaked, with the result that the ship pumped up the oil into water casks and the mixture was sold, partly in Mauritius and partly in St Helena. The Lord Chief Baron of the then Court of Exchequer said:

'they have a joint interest in the oil which was sold, and of which a common mass was made when it was pumped up. To that they are entitled as tenants in common, and you cannot ascertain how much belonging to each was lost or thrown overboard. All that was saved was sold in one mass; and it would be impossible at law to distinguish the share of the parties ... The plaintiffs have become, by the course of events, tenants in common of the oil sold. Under these circumstances it seems to me that they have a right to the account which they seek.'

In *Buckley* v. *Gross* (1863) tallow in a warehouse which was burnt down melted and flowed into a common sewer, the defendant recovered it and appropriated it to himself.

Mr Justice Blackburn said:

'The tallow of the different owners was indeed mixed up into a molten mass, so that it might be difficult to apportion it among them ... Probably the legal effect of such a mixture would be, to make the owners tenants in common in equal portions of the mass, but, at all events, they do not lose their property in it.'

Such English authority as there is therefore appears to favour the proposition that by operation of law the owners of admixed materials become joint owners as tenants in common in proportion to the value of their goods incorporated.

If that is so, even in the absence of a specific aggregation clause, Borden had a title at common law to the chipboard in *Borden* v. *Scottish Timber Products Ltd* [7.01], quite apart from their tracing rights in equity.

7.06 Contractual provisions regarding aggregation clauses

That, it is submitted, is the position in English law where there are no contractual provisions governing who is to own admixed materials. It in no way excludes express contractual provisions as to that. As Lord Justice Bridge in the *Borden* case said:

'The lesson to be learned from these conclusions is a simple one. If a seller of goods to a manufacturer, who knows that his goods are to be used in the manufacturing process before they are paid for, wishes to reserve to himself an effective security for the payment of the price, he cannot rely on a simple reservation of title clause as that relied upon by Borden.

If he wishes to acquire rights over the finished product, he can only do so by express contractual stipulation.'

Lord Justice Robert Goff in the *Clough Mill* case said:

'It is difficult to see why if the parties agree that the property in the goods shall rest in A, that agreement should not be given effect to.'

Lord Justice Oliver in the same case also said:

'I am not sure that I see any reason in principle why the original legal title in a newly manufactured article composed of materials belonging to A and B should not lie where A and B have agreed it shall lie.'

As between the parties, they are at liberty to make what contractual provisions as to the title of goods that they like and it is the duty of the courts to give effect to their contractual provisions.

7.07 Interpretation of aggregation clauses

Notwithstanding that the law is perfectly explicit that the parties can make what contractual provision they like about ownership of admixed materials, the courts have shown a remarkable and, at times, a perverse reluctance to implement aggregation clauses.

In *In re Peachdart Ltd* (1983), a receiver appointed by Barclays Bank Ltd, under its standard debenture form, applied to the Chancery Division of the High Court by summons under section 369(1) of the Companies Act 1948 (now section 492 of the Companies Act 1985) to determine whether Freudenberg Leather Co. Ltd were the owners of leather they had supplied under a retention of title clause to another company called S. Launer & Co. (London) Ltd for manufacture into handbags.

The leather was supplied under a contract which included the clause:

'(a) The risk in the Products shall pass to the Buyer (i) when the Seller delivers the Products in accordance with the terms to the Buyer or its Agent or other person to whom the Seller has been authorised by the Buyer to deliver the Products or (ii) If the Products are appropriated to the Buyer but kept at the Seller's premises at the Buyer's request AND the Seller shall have no responsibility in respect of the safety of the Products thereafter and accordingly the Buyer should insure the Products thereafter against such risks (if any) as it thinks appropriate.

(b) However the ownership of the Products shall remain with the Seller which reserves the right to dispose of the products until payment in full for all the Products has been received by it in accordance with the terms of this contract or until such time as the Buyer sells the Products to its customers by way of bona fide sale at full market value. If such payment is overdue in whole or in part the Seller may (without prejudice to any of its other rights) recover or resell the Products or any of them and may enter upon the Buyer's premises by its servants or agents for that purpose. Such payment shall become due immediately upon the commencement of any act or proceeding in which the Buyer's solvency is involved. *If any of the products are incorporated in or used as material for other goods before such payment the property in the whole of such other goods shall be and remain with the Seller until such payment has been made or the other goods have been sold as aforesaid and all the Seller's rights hereunder in the Products shall extend to those other goods.*

(c) Until the Seller is paid in full for all the Products the relationship of the Buyer to the Seller shall be fiduciary in respect of the Products or other goods in which they are incorporated or used and if the same are sold by the Buyer the Seller shall have the right to trace the proceeds thereof according to the principles in *In re Hallett's Estate* (1880) 13 Ch

D 696 [1874–80] (All E.R. Rep 793). A like right for the Seller shall apply where the Buyer uses the Products in any way so as to be entitled to payment from a third party.'

It will be seen that there was a retention of title clause; an aggregation clause and a 'proceeds of sale' clause – all drafted on the lines which were upheld in *Romalpa*.

In the receiver's possession were:

(1) some of the original unprocessed leather;
(2) completed handbags made from that leather;
(3) partly completed handbags made from that leather;
(4) the proceeds of sale of handbags made from the leather.

Mr Justice Vinelott said:

'To my mind it is impossible to suppose that in the instant case, even assuming in Freudenberg's favour that the company became a bailee of the leather when it was first delivered to it, the parties intended that until a parcel of leather had been fully paid for the company would remain a bailee of each piece of leather comprised in the parcel throughout the whole process of manufacture, that Freudenberg should have the right until the parcel had been fully paid for, to enter the company's premises and identify and take away any partly or completely manufactured handbag derived from it, and that on the sale of a completed handbag the company would be under an obligation to pay the proceeds of sale into a separate interest-bearing account and to keep them apart from their other moneys and not employ them in the trade.

It seems to me that the parties must have intended that at least after a piece of leather had been appropriated to be manufactured into a handbag and work had started on it (when the leather would cease to have any significant value as raw material) the leather would cease to be the exclusive property of Freudenberg (whether as bailor or as unpaid vendor) and that Freudenberg would thereafter have a charge on handbags in the course of manufacture and on the distinctive products which would come into existence at the end of the process of manufacture (the value of which would be derived for the most part from Mr Launer's reputation and skill in design and the skill of his work force). The charge would in due course shift to the proceeds of sale. That I accept does some violence to the language of clause 11(b) in so far as that clause provides that "The property in the whole or such other goods shall be and remain with the seller". I do not think that those words compel the conclusion that the company was to be a mere bailee throughout the whole process of manufacture until the whole purchase price of the relevant parcel had been paid, and that on a sale before that time it would be no more than an agent for Freudenberg. The language is, I think, consistent with the view that once the process of manufacture had started so that in the course of manufacture work and materials provided by the company would result in the leather being converted into (that is incorporated in or used as material for) other goods of a distinctive character the property in those other goods would vest in Freudenberg only as security for any outstanding balance of the price of the relevant parcel of leather. What the draftsman has done is to elide and I think confuse two quite different relationships.'

It is to be regretted that there was no appeal in this case, since it is clear that the judge substituted, for what the parties had actually expressed and plainly agreed, his own view of what they should have agreed. Whenever a judge says 'It seems to me that the parties must have intended . . .' one can safely conclude that he is about to do violence to what they expressly said and actually intended. In a commercial transaction a judge is supposed to give effect to the meaning of the contract. There was in this case no ambiguity whatsoever. Freudenberg Leather Co. Ltd, by the terms of their contract, retained title not only in the leather they supplied but in the handbags which were made from it. The evidence was that the fittings, consisting of thread and attachments, were of comparatively minor value.

His findings that an aggregation clause creates a charge are erroneous. Parties to a contract can make any provision they like about the title to goods or future goods, and English courts are under a constitutional obligation to uphold their contractual arrangements, however much Chancery judges may favour moneylenders.

The judge was not assisted by counsel for Freudenberg who made the entirely unnecessary and incorrect concession against the client's interest, to the effect that if it were a charge it would be void for failure to register under section 95 of the Companies Act 1948.

Happily, it must now be regarded as not being good law as the result of the observations made by the Court of Appeal in *Clough Mill* [8.12]. The same must be said of *re Andrabell Ltd* (1984) where a retention of title clause was again upheld but held to cease when the goods were processed into travel bags.

Chapter 8

Are any Retention Clauses Registrable Charges?

8.01   What is a registrable charge?

Section 95 of the Companies Act 1948 and section 395 of the current Companies Act 1985 provide that a charge created by a company over its property shall be registered in the Company Registry within twenty-one days or it will be void against a liquidator of the company and any creditor, if it falls into one of the three categories specified in section 396 of the 1985 Act.

   The full terms of the sections are set out in [8.02] but the following observations may be made here.

(a)   The charge must be over the company's property *or undertaking*

It has been held that the charge does not need to cover the whole of the company's undertaking on property (although that was probably the original intention of the draftsman), but may be over part of it, such as the company's goods: *Mercantile Bank of India Ltd* v. *Chartered Bank of India Australia and China* (1938).

   In the High Court in the *Romalpa* case it was contended that the retention of title clause constituted a charge over the company's goods.

   This was dismissed briefly by Mr Justice Mocatta with the words:

'If the property in the foil never passed to the defendants ... section 95(1) had no application.'

The issue was not raised in the Court of Appeal for self-evident reasons. Nobody can create a charge over other people's property.

   In spite of that, the trial judge in *Clough Mill* (1984) held that because the purpose of the retention of title clause was to ensure payment to the supplier, it constituted a charge. The Court of Appeal swiftly corrected that fallacy. If ownership of the goods had never passed to the company, it could not possibly create a charge over them.

(b) The charge must be one that is 'created by the company'

It is stretching the meaning of the words too far to suggest, as Mr Justice Slade did, in *In re Bond Worth Ltd,* that the company which received goods subject to a retention of title clause created a charge.

(c) The obligation in law is upon the company itself to register the charge

Section 399 of the Companies Act 1985 reads:

> '(1) It is the company's duty to send to the registrar of companies for registration the particulars of every charge created by the company ... (3) If a company fails to comply with subsection (1) then unless the registration has been effected on the application of some other person, *the company and every officer of it who is in default is liable to a fine, and for continued contravention to a daily default fine.*'

The Act provides for registration of a charge 'on the application of any person interested in it', but imposes no obligations whatsoever on any person to do so. It is only the company and its officers who are under the statutory obligation.

It will be suggested in due course [9.03] that a company's failure to register a charge will estop the company from setting up its own criminal default so as to defeat a charge: and that a receiver is in no better position in this respect than the company itself.

(d) The charge, even if unregistered is still binding inter partes, *that is between the company and the creditor who holds the charge*

This was made clear in *Independent Automative Sales Ltd* v. *Knowles & Foster* (1962). As will be seen, a receiver is in no better position than the company and section 395(2) makes specific provisions for repayment.

(e) An unregistered charge is void only against 'the liquidator or other creditors'.

A receiver appointed by a secured creditor is neither.

(f) An unregistered charge is void only in the event of a liquidation

Consequently, if the charge is realised by the creditor before the company is wound up that creditor obtains an impregnable title, good against both liquidator and other creditors. Only in the event of liquidation does section 395 come into operation, and nothing done before that can stop the company paying off a secured but unregistered charge or prevent the holder of that charge from enforcing his security: *re Cardiff Workmen's Cottage Co. Ltd* (1906).

The Act specifically provides that the expression 'a charge' shall include 'a mortgage'. A mortgage is the transfer of the legal title in property to a lender, as security for a loan, the title to be transferred back to the borrower when full payment has been made. A charge is a form of security which entitles a creditor to receive payment out of the proceeds of specific property.

8.02 Requirements of the Companies Act 1985

The relevant terms of the statute are:

395.—(1) Subject to the provision of this Chapter, a charge created by a company registered in England and Wales and being a charge to which this section applies is, so far as any security on the company's property or undertaking is conferred by the charge, void against the liquidator and any creditor of the company, unless the prescribed particulars of the charge together with the instrument (if any) by which the charge is created or evidenced, are delivered to or received by the registrar of companies for registration in the manner required by this Chapter within 21 days after the date of the charge's creation.

(2) Subsection (1) is without prejudice to any contract or obligation for repayment of the money secured by the charge; and when a charge becomes void under this section, the money secured by it immediately becomes payable.

396.—(1) Section 395 applies to the following charges—

  . . .

  . . .

  (*c*) a charge created or evidenced by an instrument which, if executed by an individual, would require registration as a bill of sale,

  . . .

  (*e*) a charge on book debts of the company,

(*f*) a floating charge on the company's undertaking or property,

It will be seen therefore that if any retention of title clause, current account clause or aggregation clause should constitute a charge it is only registrable if it falls into one of the three relevant categories.

8.03 Registration within twenty-one days of creation

Section 95 of the Companies Act 1948 and section 395 of the Companies Act 1985 provide that charges created by a company as are required to be registered shall be registered with the Registrar of Companies within twenty-one days of their creation. The appropriate document is Form 27.

For many years it was the practice of the Registrar, where a Form 27 was submitted within twenty-one days but was defective in some way, for him to return it for correction and to accept it subsequently, even outside the twenty-one day period.

However, it has now been decided that this practice had no authority in law, and that a defective form submitted within the twenty-one days is not registration under the Act.

As a result, the Registrar decided he had no authority to accept defective forms. In particular, he would reject forms which did not correctly describe the *instrument* which created the charge, which did not set out the *amount* due, or adequately describe *the property* to be charged. He requested that forms submitted should be sent to Companies House, Cardiff or Companies House, City Road, London, marked 'Mortgage Section'.

If the charge is not registered within twenty-one days, section 101 of the 1948 Act and section 404 of the 1985 Act empowers the High Court to extend the time for registration provided that failure to register was 'accidental or due to misadventure or some other sufficient clause'.

Presumably these words are wide enough to cover the situation whereby, due to an obscure state of the law, it was widely believed that registration was not necessary; but there is no specific authority on this point.

8.04 Late registration of charges

The High Court has had, since the Companies Act 1900, power to allow a charge or mortgage to be registered outside the period of twenty-one days allowed.

The present law is currently contained in section 401 of the Companies Act 1985 and reads:

'(1) The following applies if the court is satisfied that the omission to register a charge within the time required by this Chapter or that the omission or mis-statement of any particular with respect to any such charge or in a memorandum of satisfaction was accidental, or due to inadvertence or to some other sufficient cause, or is not of a nature to prejudice the position of creditors or shareholders of the company, or that on other grounds it is just and equitable to grant relief.

(2) The court may, on the application of the company or a person interested, and on such terms and conditions as seem to the court just and expedient, order that the time for registration shall be extended or, as the case may be, that the omission or mis-statement shall be rectified.

It therefore appears possible for a supplier with a retention of title clause that a receiver contends is void for failure to register under section 395 of the 1985 Act or section 95 of the 1948 Act, to apply to the court for registration out of time, if the Court should find it to be a registrable charge.

It must surely be 'just and equitable' to grant such relief on the grounds that the decisions of Chancery judges have turned the simple common law into 'a maze if not a minefield', so that it is impossible for any businessman to know what retention clauses are registrable and what are not.

Alternatively, the failure to register could be 'accidental or due to inadvertence or some other sufficient cause'. A 'sufficient cause' must surely be the mess the judges have made of the law.

There is no requirement that late registration should not be of such a nature to prejudice the position of creditors or shareholders. That clause is a disjunctive and alternative, and on proper construction of the section, it should be taken to indicate since it is a separate ground, that even if creditors and shareholders are prejudiced, that is no ground for refusing relief.

In all cases, therefore, where a receiver applies to the High Court under section 369(1) of the Companies Act 1948 or section 492(1) of the Companies Act 1985 there should therefore be a counter summons by the supplier for leave to register the charge out of time, if it is held to be one by the court.

8.05   Charges created by operation of the law are not required to be registered under the Companies Act

In the Court of Appeal it was expressly made clear in *Capital Finance Co.*

Ltd v. *Stokes* (1969) and *London Cheshire Co. Ltd* v. *Laplagrene Co. Ltd* (1971) that a charge, such as an unpaid seller's lien, does not require registration under section 95 of the Companies Act.

In the latter case, the statement in *Buckley on the Companies Acts*, 13th ed. (1957), page 213, was quoted:

> '*Semble*, a right given by the general law such as a vendor's or solicitor's lien, is not a charge 'created' by the company and does not therefore require registration.'

Palmer's Company Law, 21st ed. (1968), page 413, was also quoted in the same case:

> 'But a lien which is not created but which arises by operation of law (e.g. a solicitor's or a vendor's lien) need not, it is submitted, be registered, since registration is only required in the case of charges created after the fixed date.'

Both statements were expressly approved by the Court.

Mr Justice Brightman concluded:

> 'The enactment in question has been in force since the Companies Act 1908, and no one has suggested ... that it is the practice for a vendor to register an unpaid vendor's lien merely because he is selling to a company.
>
> If such a lien is registrable, the time for registration would expire twenty-one days after the exchange of contracts for sale, because it is at that date that the lien is created; it is not created on completion because the purchase price is unpaid; but is discharged on completion to the extent that the purchase money is paid: *In re Birmingham, decd* (1959).
>
> In most cases, the twenty-one day period would expire well before completion, because contracts for sale of land are not usually completed in three weeks.
>
> It would be a profound inconvenience therefore if every vendor to a company were compelled as a matter of course to register an unpaid vendor's lien.
>
> For my part, I am content to rely on the dictum of Harman LJ in the *Capital Finance* case (1969) that an unpaid vendor's lien is the creature of the law; and that it does not depend upon contract, but upon the fact that the vendor has a right to specific performance of his contract. This was also the view expressed by Lawrence, LJ in *In re Bernstein* (1925):

There is in my opinion an essential distinction between a mortgage and a vendor's lien; the former is a security upon real or personal property for the payment of a debt, or for the performance of an engagement, created by contract between the parties; whereas the latter is a charge arising by the law.'

The unpaid seller of goods is in no different position than the unpaid seller of real estate. If he sells to a company there is no need for him to register his lien, it is submitted.

8.06   Equitable rights of unpaid sellers

An unpaid seller has either a lien or a charge over property which arises by operation of law and equity and these require no registration under the Companies Acts.

An unpaid seller is defined by section 38 of the Sale of Goods Act 1979 as one where the whole of the price has not been paid or where a bill of exchange (including a cheque) or other negotiable instrument accepted for the goods has not been honoured.

Even though ownership has passed to the buyer, the seller is entitled to retain the goods until payment: section 39(1)(a). And he is entitled to resell them in accordance with the provisions set out in section 48.

If he has parted with the goods and they are in transit to the buyer when the buyer becomes insolvent, the seller also is entitled to stop them in transit and repossess them; section 39(1)(b): section 44.

If the property in the goods has not passed to the buyer, the seller is entitled to withhold delivery until payment is made by the buyer. That was the position at common law long before the Sale of Goods Act 1893 was passed. The rule is now incorporated in section 39(2) of the Sale of Goods Act 1979.

If the unpaid seller relinquishes possession of the goods to the seller, in substitution for his lien he is given an equitable charge over the goods.

Moreover, any unpaid seller with an equitable charge over the property will take priority over a receiver and debenture holders, whatever the nature or wording of the instrument by which the receiver was appointed.

In *Wilson* v. *Kelland* (1910) the Bedford Brewery (Plymouth) Ltd executed in 1901 a trust deed in favour of the Law Guarantee and Trust Society which was in effect a debenture with floating charge over all the company's assets, present and future, with a mortgage of specific properties. It provided that the brewery company 'shall not be at liberty to create any mortgage or charge on such premises ranking in priority to or *in pari passu* with the security created in favour of the debentures'.

Three years later, in 1904, the company agreed to buy a brewery from A. & W. Kelland for £5350 and it was a term of the agreement that £3000 should remain on mortgage. Conveyance of the premises took place in September 1904 with the creation of a legal mortgage in favour of the Kellands for £3000 on 27 January 1905.

Mr Justice Eve held that it was immaterial whether, at the time when that mortgage was created, the mortgagees had notice of the debentures of 1901.

> 'Any equity which attached to the property contracted to be purchased was, throughout, subject to the paramount equity of the unpaid vendors. The legal mortgage which secures the unpaid purchase-moneys must, in my opinion, take priority over any charge ... to persons claiming through the company.'

He made an order against the company and their debenture holders for foreclosure. It is noteworthy that in that case the debenture concerned had been properly registered under section 14 of the Companies Act 1900, which was in similar terms to section 95 of the Companies Act 1948. The mortgage which took priority to it had not been registered.

The principle appears to be that an unpaid seller who has parted with the legal title has a lien on the property, whether it is real estate or a chattel. This right in respect of goods is expressly preserved by the Sale of Goods Act 1979, section 39(1)(a):

> 'notwithstanding that the property in the goods has passed to the buyer, the unpaid seller can exercise his lien so long as the goods are in his possession.'

If he relinquishes possession in exchange for a promise of an equitable charge over the goods, that equitable charge takes priority over any other equitable charge, even if created earlier and registered. This is because the company has in fact only acquired the 'equity of redemption': that is, the right to acquire beneficial ownership on the paying off of the charge. Debenture holders and their receiver can never be in a better position than the company and therefore they are subject to such a charge.

That is made abundantly clear from *In re Connolly Brothers Ltd (No. 2)* (1912). The company had debentures, issued in 1901 and, again, registered under the Companies Act 1900, which created a floating charge on their whole undertaking and all property present and future. One of the conditions of the debenture was that the company should not be at liberty to create any mortgage or charge in priority to the debentures. In 1904, the company wanted to buy some property in Manchester but had no funds available. The directors therefore asked a Mrs O'Reilly to lend them £1000 to enable them to purchase it for £1050, and promised her a charge on the property to secure the sum to be advanced. She agreed and the conveyance took place. The company subsequently gave Mrs O'Reilly's solicitor, who held the title deeds, a memorandum in which it acknowledged that he held the deeds with intent by the company to create an equitable charge on the property and an undertaking to execute a legal mortgage if called upon so to do. This charge was not registered under the Companies Act, or elsewhere.

Later it was claimed that the debentures took priority. Mr Justice Warrington held that Mrs O'Reilly's unregistered charge took priority over the debentures. He said that her case could be put in either of two ways:

'By virtue of the doctrine of subrogation, she stands in the place of the vendor and therefore has the benefit of the vendor's lien. She did not advance this money unconditionally. She agreed to make this advance for the purpose and sole purpose of paying off the purchase money and under a contemporaneous agreement that she was to have a charge on the property.'

The second way of putting it, he found, was conclusive:

'The debentures, so far as this after-acquired property is concerned, amount to nothing more than a contract by the company to give the debenture holders a security upon that particular item of property ... but only on such interest as the company may in fact acquire ...

The company never acquired ... any interest in this property at all – except subject to an obligation to give Mrs O'Reilly a charge ...

The security acquired by Mrs O'Reilly takes priority over the debentures because it takes priority over the interest of the company itself ... Nothing was subject to the trust deed except what one may describe as the "equity of redemption"...'

The Court of Appeal unanimously approved this judgment. Lord Cozens-Hardy, MR said:

'All the company in equity obtained was the equity of redemption in the property, subject to Mrs O'Reilly's charge.'

Lord Justice Buckley said,

'If the company obtained the property, subject to a contractual obligation to give a first charge on it to Mrs O'Reilly, then the debenture holders can get no more.'

Once again an unregistered charge prevailed over registered debentures.

The same principle was upheld by the Privy Council, (Lord Cross of Chelsea, Lord Simon of Glaisdale and Lord Edmund-Davies) in *Security Trust Co.* v. *The Royal Bank of Canada* (1976).

The facts are more complex but the judicial committee unanimously approved the decision in *In re Connolly Brothers Ltd*, and for the same reasons. Once again an unregistered mortgage was given priority over a registered debenture.

That being so, one may well wonder why effect was not given to this doctrine in *In re Bond Worth Ltd*. In that case, the judge held that legal title in the goods was transferred to the buyers on the condition that they held the title subject to beneficial ownership of the unpaid sellers. He held that this amounted to a charge by way of security, but he went on to hold that it was void against the receiver for the debenture holders because it was not registered under section 95 of the Companies Act 1948.

His explanation for not applying the principle of *In re Connolly Brothers Ltd* is contained in these words:

'Though this argument has some superficial attraction, I do not think that the *Connolly* decision, when properly analysed, is of any assistance to Monsanto.

As will have appeared, that was a case where A, the purchaser of the relevant property from B, had, before completion, entered into a contract for good consideration, to grant a charge over the property in favour of C. Accordingly, the very moment that A acquired the legal estate in the property, A held it in trust to give effect in equity to C's rights, by virtue of the pre-existing contract between A and C.

In the face of this contract, it could not therefore have been successfully claimed that the purchaser A, even for a moment, acquired more than an equity of redemption in the property, (though it may be observed that the relevant charge, even in that case, was undeniably created by A, rather than the vendor B).

The case did not even touch the question whether it would have been conceptually possible for the vendor B to except to himself a mortgage in such a manner that the subject matter of the sale, as between A and B, was a mere equity of redemption, so that the transaction involved no express or implied grant back by A in favour of B.

Notwithstanding the arrangements made between A and C, the

transaction as between A and B in the *Connolly* case remains throughout one for the sale of the entire legal and beneficial interest in the property.'

With respect to Mr Justice Slade, as he then was, it is difficult to follow his argument. Quite apart from the fact that his construction of the contract was contrary to its plain meaning, he adopted the view throughout that the legal and equitable position regarding the sale of goods was no different from that of real property. The rights of Mrs O'Reilly were second-hand rights in that she was subrogated to, or in ordinary language, stood in the shoes of, the original unpaid vendor. She therefore had the same rights that he would have had.

It is instructive therefore to revert to the case which is the closest analogy to that before him in *In re Bond Worth Ltd*, namely, *Wilson* v. *Kelland*, to which his lordship was referred but which he did not discuss in his judgment. In *Wilson* v. *Kelland*, a vendor relinquished his lien as unpaid seller over property he had agreed to sell for £5350 in return for £2530 and a contractual promise that he would be granted an equitable charge over the property of £3000. The charge which was subsequently created was unregistered but was held to prevail over an earlier created and registered floating charge over all the assets, present or future of the company. The reason for this was that the company had only acquired an equity of redemption for the property.

In *In re Bond Worth Ltd*, the vendor relinquished his lien as unpaid seller over property he had agreed to sell for over £500,000 in return for a contractual promise that he would remain beneficial owner of the goods; which his lordship held to be an equitable charge, created by the purchaser in favour of the vendor, for the whole of the purchase price. Why then, *vis-a-vis* the debenture holders and their receivers (who had no greater rights than the company itself), were they not deferred to the equitable rights of the unpaid seller?

The argument from the *Connolly* decision is not superficially attractive but entirely logical and convincing. The legal position can be stated in simple propositions:

Proposition 1: A seller who has agreed to sell real or personal property to a buyer has a lien (a right) to retain the property until he is paid in full by the buyer, even though the ownership of the property has by contract, under English law, passed to the buyer.

Proposition 2: If, in reliance on the contractual promise of a company (the buyer), that it will enter into an obligation to pay the full agreed price and will, until payment, grant to the unpaid seller an equitable charge on the property, the unpaid seller relinquishes his lien on the goods, the company will acquire the legal title to the property solely subject to the rights of the unpaid seller. These rights must, as a matter of law and equity, prevail over any debenture, whatever its terms, registered before the transaction for the simple reason that all the company has acquired is merely the right to acquire beneficial ownership to accompany its legal ownership on payment of the full purchase price.

Proposition 3: The debenture holders, and their receiver, can never have greater rights than the company itself has. If the company has acquired by contract only the legal title to the goods, subject to the rights of the unpaid seller, the receiver has no greater rights.

Proposition 4: In all this, it is irrelevant whether or not the equity of the real owner is registered or not. If a company buys only the shell of a crab, the debenture holders, through the receiver, cannot claim its contents. The rights of the debenture holders attach only to the shell.

Therefore, if a company acquires the legal title to goods subject to an equitable charge for the whole of the purchase price, a receiver appointed by the debenture holders can never acquire more than the equity of redemption, i.e. the right to become owner in law and in equity by paying the unpaid seller in full for the goods.

This, however, is not what Mr Justice Slade decided in *In re Bond Worth Ltd*. He held that the unpaid seller's equitable interest in the goods and their proceeds constituted a floating charge which must have been properly registered under section 95 of the Companies Act 1948, if it were to prevail against a receiver appointed on behalf of earlier debenture holders.

It is therefore necessary to examine in detail what charges are required to be registered under section 95 of the 1948 Act and sections 395 and 396 of the Companies Act 1985.

Even if Mr Justice Slade were correct in holding that the retention of title clause in *In re Bond Worth Ltd* amounted only to a charge, how did it become a registrable one? Into which category did it fall? And in which category did the charge allegedly created by the aggregation clause in *In re Peachdart* fall?

There are only three classes of created charges which require registration: floating charges, charges on book debts and those which, if created by an individual, would require registering as a bill of sale. It is submitted that these charges, if charges they be, do not fall into any of these categories [8.07], [8.08], [8.09].

8.07 Is a retention clause a floating charge?

From the wording of the statutes, the floating charge has to be on the company's undertaking or property. Although one would think from the wording that such a charge would have to be over the whole of the company's business and assets to be charged by the section, it has been held that it applies to floating charges over part only of a company's assets: *Mercantile Bank of India* v. *Chartered Bank of India* (1930).

But as Lord Justice Robert Goff observed in the Court of Appeal in the course of arguments in the *Clough Mill* case: 'How can a charge over *goods* created by a retention clause possibly be a *floating* charge?' He did not receive any answer from the respondent's counsel.

The essence of a floating charge is that it floats in the air unattached to specific assets or property until the happening of a specific event, when it descends like a hangman's noose.

Clearly, whether a retention of title clause is a charge or not, it is not one that requires to be registered under 95(2)(f) of the 1948 Companies Act or 396(f) of the 1985 Companies Act.

A floating charge was defined in the case of *In re Florence Land and Public Works Company ex parte Moor* (1878) as one which is:

'on the property of the company as a going concern, subject to the powers of the directors to dispose of the property of the company while carrying on its business in the ordinary course.'

In the same case Lord Justice James said it is a charge on 'the assets for the time being' of the company, and does not prevent the company carrying on its business.

So it was held in the case before Mr Justice North of *Wheatley* v. *Silkstone and Haigh Moor Coal Company* (1885).

8.08   Is a retention clause a charge over book debts?

The answer to this one is simple: How can a charge over *goods* possibly be a charge over *debts*? Even if a 'proceeds of sale' clause is written into the contract, the requirements of section 95(2)(e) of the 1948 Act and section 396(1)(e) of the 1985 Act relate only to *existing* book debts, i.e. money that is due to the company at the date when the charge is created by an instrument of some sort: *Paul and Frank Ltd* v. *Discount Bank (Overseas) Ltd* (1967). It has no application to *future* book debts.

At one time when there was no obligation on a company to keep books, it was thought that any debts which could have been entered in *books* were to be regarded as 'book debts' by the predecessor section.

However, in the *Paul and Frank Ltd* case, Mr Kenneth Cork (then unknighted), the liquidator of that company, claimed that a letter of authority given to the Export Credit Guarantee Department constituted the creation of a book debt in future and should have been registered under section 95 and was therefore void against him.

Four chartered accountants testified that at the date of the letter of authority, it ought not to have been entered in to the company's accounts as a 'book debt'.

Mr Justice Pennywick said:

'Looking at the matter for a moment apart from authority, I do not think that in ordinary speech one would describe as a "book debt" the right under a contingency contract before the contingency happens. By "contingency contract" in this connection, I mean contracts of insurance, guarantee, indemnity and the like.'

He then referred to the cases of *Shipley* v. *Marshall* (1863) and *Independent Automatic Sales Ltd* v. *Knowles & Foster* (1962) and said:

'Section 95 requires registration of a charge on book debts within twenty-one days of creation. It seems to me that, in order to ascertain whether any particular charge is a charge on book debts within the meaning of the section, one must look at the items of property which form the subject matter of the charge at the date of its creation and consider whether any of those items is a book debt.

In the case of an existing item of property, this question can only be answered by reference to its character at the date of creation.

Where the item of property is the benefit of a contract and at the date of the charge the benefit of the contract does not comprehend any book debt, I do not see how that contract can be brought within the section as being a book debt merely by reason that the contract may ultimately result in a book debt.

Here, the E.C.G. policy admittedly did not comprehend any book debt at the date of the letter of authority, and that seems to me to be an end of the matter.'

He later added:

'It by no means follows ... that paragraph (e) applies to an existing contract which does not comprehend a book debt merely by reason that that contract may result in a book debt in the future.'

From this, it is clear that the fact that a retention clause has a 'proceeds of sale' provision does not make it subject to the statutes, since there is no 'book debt' existing at the date of the contract.

The case of *Independent Automatic Sales Limited* v. *Knowles & Foster* (1962) is not authority to the contrary, although so stated by *Palmer's Company Law* in the 1967 edition Volume 1 p. 596. In that case, a retail company which sold goods under hire purchase agreements expressly charged the agreements with responsibility for the discharge of a loan. It was held that this was a registrable charge.

A sale of future hire purchase agreements was held to be a charge on book debts by Mr Justice Eve, but he was reversed on this point by the Court of Appeal in *re George Inglefield Limited* (1933). This was followed in *Lloyds & Scottish Finance Limited* v. *Prentice* (1977), and confirmed by the House of Lords in *Lloyds & Scottish Finance Limited* v. *Cyril Lord Carpet Sales Limited* in 1979.

Two reasons were given in these cases. First, the outright assignment of future hire purchase agreements were absolute assignments of customers' debts and not mere charges on them, even though in the *Lloyds & Scottish Finance* cases the bank was only entitled to 80 per cent of them. It was a sale of a future book debt charge.

Second, to be a registrable charge within the meaning of the statutes there had to be in existence at the time when the charge was created an *existing* book debt; there cannot be one where the 'book debt' comes into existence at some time in the future, dependent on a contingency which may or may not happen.

Moreover, for many years it has been established law that an agreement to create a charge, whatever its nature, in the future is operative only when that charge is in fact created and is it not registrable therefore until then: *In re Gregory Love & Co.* (1915); *re Columbian Fireproofing Co. Ltd* (1910). Especially this is so when the creation of the charge is contingent upon an event which may or may not happen, e.g. the sale of goods entrusted to a retailer as a bailee for the unpaid seller who has a retention of title clause.

The position was admirably explained by Professor Pennington in the 4th edition of his book, *Company Law*, p. 423:

'If a company purchases goods on terms that they shall remain the property of the seller until the purchase price is paid and that if the company resells the goods, it shall do so as agent for the seller and the re-sale price payable by the sub-purchaser shall belong to the seller, the company does not thereby create a charge over the re-sale price and so the agreement is not registrable as a charge on its book debts. Both the goods and the claim for the re-sale price belongs throughout to the original seller and no security is created over assets belonging to the company. This is so even if the company is entitled to any surplus of the re-sale price over the amount it owes the seller and even though the seller has agreed to allow the company time for payment of the original sale price.'

But in any event, the outright assignment of part of a book debt, present or future, is not registrable: *Ashby Warner & Co.* v. *Simmons* (1936).

8.09   Is a retention of title clause subject to the Bills of Sale Acts?

Bills of sale apply only to individuals and not to companies: *re Standard Manufacturing Co.* (1891). They are documents whereby the owner of a chattel transfers title of the goods to another person while he remains in possession of them.

There are two classes of bills of sale. The first class are those where the property in the goods is transferred absolutely to the third person. This can be by way of sale or gift.

The second and more common kind is where the bill of sale is by way of mortgage with the legal title to the goods transferred to another by way of security, subject to the term that the transferor becomes the owner again on repayment of the monies lent. This latter case is specifically dealt with under the Bills of Sale Act (1878) (Amendment) Act 1882.

Every bill of sale must be attested and registered at the central office of the Supreme Court within seven days of execution and must specify the consideration for which it is given. If not registered, the bills are valid between the parties but are void against any creditor who has obtained judgment from a court, or a trustee in bankruptcy.

There are therefore three essential elements to constitute a bill of sale.

(a) The person executing it must be the owner of the goods. For this reason, the ordinary simple retention of title clause cannot possibly be a bill of sale for the simple reason that the whole purpose of it is to ensure that the prospective buyer does not become the owner until he has paid for the goods.
(b) The Bills of Sale Acts 1878–1891 apply only to *documents* whereby title is transferred and not to other transactions. Hence, if the admixture of goods creates a charge it cannot possibly be a charge which is required to be registered.
(c) Bills of sale can only be created by individuals and not by companies.

However, as has been seen [8.02], section 396 of the Companies Act 1985 requires the registration of a charge 'created or evidenced by *an instrument* which if executed by an individual, would require registration as a bill of sale'.

But not every instrument which may create a charge is a bill of sale. Excluded are pledges of the goods or documents of title to the goods; and also any document which effects the transfer of goods 'in the ordinary course of business'.

8.10   The Bills of Sale Acts

The Bills of Sale Acts 1878–1891 apply only to *documents* and not to other transactions. If therefore the admixture of goods creates a charge, it is one to which the Bills of Sale Acts have no application whatsoever.

A Bill of sale is defined in section 4 of the 1878 Act thus:

'The expression "bill of sale" shall include assignments, transfers, declarations of trust without transfer, inventories of goods with receipt attached thereto, or receipts for purchase-money of goods, and other assurances of personal chattels ... authorities or licences to take possession of personal chattels as security for any debt, and also any agreement, whether intended or not to be followed by the execution of any other instrument, by which a right in equity to any personal chattels or to any charge or security thereon shall be conferred; *but shall not include the following documents ... transfers of goods in the ordinary course of business of any trade or calling* ... bills of lading, India warrants, warehouse keepers' certificates, warrants or orders for the delivery of goods, or any other documents used in the ordinary course of business as proof of the possession or control of goods, or authorising or purporting to authorise, either by indorsement or by delivery, the possessor of such document to transfer or receive goods thereby represented.'

The exceptions are important. In *re Young, Hamilton & Co. ex parte Carter* (1904), a Manchester partnership of textile merchants were in the practice of shipping goods to India. They sold only against orders, purchased the goods with money provided by the National Bank of India Ltd and sent them first to bleachers and dyers and provided the bank with what was described as 'a letter of hypothecation' – in other words, one that created a charge over the goods in favour of the bank for 'a loan on the security of goods in preparation for shipment to the East'.

The material parts of their standard letter read:

'We beg to advise having drawn a cheque on you for £——, which amount please place to the debit of our loan account No. 2 as a loan on the security of goods in course of preparation for shipment to the East.

As security for this advance we hold on your account and under lien to you the undermentioned goods in the hands of [here followed a list of goods and names of bleachers] as per their receipt inclosed.

These goods when ready will be shipped to Calcutta, and the bills of lading duly indorsed will be handed to you, and we then undertake to repay the above advance either in cash or from the proceeds of our drafts on Messrs Ewing & Co., Calcutta to be negotiated by you and secured by the shipping documents representing the above-mentioned goods.'

The partnership was made bankrupt and the trustee in bankruptcy claimed that the letters constituted bills of sale within the meaning of section 4 and were void because they were not registered. It was, it was claimed 'a clear declaration of trust without transfer of the goods' and 'an authority or licence to take possession of chattels as security for a debt' and also 'an agreement by which a right in equity to personal chattels or to a charge or security thereon is conferred'. *Ex parte Parsons* (1886) was relied upon.

It may, perhaps, have been all these things, but the Court held that under section 4 of the Bills of Sale Act 1878 it was 'a transfer of goods in the ordinary course of business'. It also held that the document was one 'used in the ordinary course of business as proof of the control of goods'. So, too, it would appear is the ordinary commercial invoice.

It will be noted that the statute uses a wider term than 'sale', namely 'transfer', and a wider term than either ownership or possession, namely 'control'.

Clearly, no retention of title clause, however worded, can possibly come within the scope of section 95(2)(c) of the 1948 Act or section 396(1) of the 1985 Act.

8.11 Companies and the Bills of Sale Acts

Sections 4 and 5 of the Bills of Sale Act (1878) Amendment Act 1882 also provide that a bill of sale given by an individual is void, except as against that individual, if it purports to include future goods. Therefore charges over future goods are in no circumstances registrable.

It has been suggested that this rule does not apply to bills of sale given by companies and observations made by Lord Parker of Waddington and Lord Sumner in *Dublin City Distillery* v. *Doherty* (1914) are advanced as supporting this proposition. Neither opinion does in fact do so. Companies cannot execute bills of sale and the Acts deal exclusively with individuals.

The Companies Act 1985 requires, however, registration under Section 396(c) 'if a charge created or evidenced by an instrument which if executed by an individual would require registration as a Bill of Sale'.

The *Dublin City Distillery* case was, in part, concerned with warrants issued to one of its directors, in exchange for a loan, whereby certain specified casks of whisky were described as 'deliverable' to him. The whisky was undoubtedly originally the property of Dublin City Distillery. The rules of the Customs and Excise at that time authorised the distillers to transfer ownership to another person, while the whisky was in bond, but thereafter only the transferee could obtain delivery out of bond on payment of the excise duty; in short, they would not allow any further or subsequent sales in bond.

Dublin City Distillers retained the right to sell the whisky described in the warrants as 'deliverable' to the plaintiff and to other people and for that reason his name was entered only in pencil against the casks in their stock ledger. Casks 'deliverable' to him were with his consent in fact sold to other persons and in that event the Excise were advised. The plaintiff was credited with other casks of whisky in lieu.

When the company became insolvent, the plaintiff contended that this was a good and valid pledge at common law on the whiskies standing in his name.

A pledge is a transaction whereby the pledgee comes into possession of the pledger's goods in return for a loan, with the obligation to restore them if and when the pledgor repays the loan, needless to say, with interest. Pawnbrokers, familiar characters in Balzac and Dickens, are familiar examples of pledgees. Before there can be a pledge, however, the owner of the goods must have possession of them which he entrusts to the pledgee.

It was argued that there had been a constructive rendering up of possession by the plaintiff by the warrants so that Dublin City Distillers had thereby not only passed property in the casks of whisky to the plaintiff but had also yielded up possession. Various cases were quoted in which the seller of goods, who had remained in possession of them with the consent of the buyer, had thereby become a bailee of them for him.

It is not surprising, therefore, that all four Lords of Appeal apparently (although their opinions are obscure) held this was no common law pledge since the casks of whisky had never come into the physical or constructive possession of the plaintiff. Very much as a subsidiary point it was argued that if it were not a pledge, the warrants constituted a bill of sale which because it was not registered under section 14 of the Companies Act 1900 (corresponding loosely to s.396(1)(c) of the Companies Act 1985) was void against a liquidator.

What Lord Parker said, at p. 854 was:

> 'Assuming the warrants to have been bills of sale, would they, if executed by an individual, have required registration as bills of sale? If bills of sale, they would, if executed by an individual have been totally void under the Irish Bills of Sale Act 1883 for at least three reasons: they are not in the statutory form required for all bills of sale by way of security for money; they are not attested; and, they do not state the consideration for which they were given. They would be no more valid if registered than unregistered. They could not, therefore, require registration in any ordinary sense of the word. At the same time it is hardly conceivable that s.14 sub-s.1(c) was intended only to refer to instruments which fulfilled these statutory requirements. I think, therefore, that the provision therein contained must be construed as applying to all instruments which, if executed by an individual, would for their validity require registration, apart from any other ground upon which they would be invalid under the Irish Bills of Sale Act of 1883. If this be so the warrants, if bills of sale at all, would be within s.14 sub-section 1(c) of the Companies Act 1900.

It will be noted that he did not in fact suggest that the warrants were in fact bills of sale, and that his comments were entirely *obiter dicta*.

Lord Sumner, alone of all the four law lords, said:

> 'That the security in this case was a "charge created or evidenced" by so-called warrants, which "if executed by an individual would require registration as a bill of sale", within the Companies Act 1900, s.14(1)(c), I make no doubt. The question then is whether it is a document which, if executed by a natural person, would require registration as a bill of sale. The mere fact that the transaction could not be expressed in the statutory form prescribed for bills of sale is beside the point. The statutory requirement of registration of a document issued by a company cannot be defeated merely because a similar document between other parties would have been void on other grounds.
>
> In my opinion these warrants come at any rate within the words in s.4 of the Bills of Sale (Ireland) Act 1879:

> > "Any agreement ... by which a right in equity to any personal chattels, or to any charge or security thereon, shall be conferred".

They may also be "assurances of personal chattels" or "authorities or licences to take possession of personal chattels as security for any debt". The question turns on the wording of these instruments themselves and the circumstances under which they were created in this case.

In my opinion these documents are void for want of registration and upon this part of the case the appeal must succeed.'

None of this is authority for the proposition that companies are subject to different rules about bills of sale than are individuals.

8.12   An ordinary retention clause is no charge

Clough Mill Ltd v. *Geoffrey Martin* was a common law action for conversion brought against the receiver appointed by a bank to a company called Heatherdale Fabric Ltd, to whom the plaintiffs had supplied yarn. Since plaintiffs always have a choice of forum, it is difficult to understand how the case ended up in the Manchester Chancery Court.

The plaintiffs at all material times knew that their yarn was to be spun into fabric by Heatherdale. The yarn was supplied on the following express terms:

'However, the ownership of the material shall remain with the Seller, which reserves the right to dispose of the material until payment in full for all the material has been received by it in accordance with the terms of this contract or until such time as the Buyer sells the material to its customers by way of bona fide sale at full market value.

If such payment is overdue in whole or in part the Seller may (without prejudice to any of its other rights) recover or re-sell the material or any of it and may enter upon the Buyer's premises by its servants or agents for that purpose.

Such payment shall become due immediately upon the commencement of any act or proceeding in which the Buyer's solvency is involved.

If any of the material is incorporated in or used as material for other goods before such payment the property in the whole of such goods shall be and remain with the Seller until such payment has been made, or the other goods have been sold as aforesaid, and all the Seller's rights hereunder in the material shall extend to those other goods.'

It will be seen, therefore, that the condition comprised:

(a) a simple retention of title clause [4.01];
(b) a current account clause [4.03];

(c) an aggregation clause [4.06].

There were other provisions, one of which excluded any equitable right of set-off and another passed the risk to the prospective buyer on delivery. Also:

'(a) The price payable for the material shall be net and payment shall be made within the period stated overleaf.

. . .

(c) The Seller shall be entitled to suspend or cancel further deliveries under this or any other contracts between the parties hereto: (i) if any payment is overdue ...
(d) For the purpose of this condition, time of payment shall be of the essence of the contract.
(e) The Buyer shall not be entitled to withhold or set-off payment for material delivered for any reason whatsoever.'

These well-drafted provisions had not been devised by Clough Mill Ltd; they were in fact 'borrowed' from Courtaulds who had had them in use for many years. There was no financial link between Clough Mill and Courtaulds.

On 11th March 1980, Lloyds Bank appointed Geoffrey Martin as receiver of Heatherdale. At that time Heatherdale owed part of the purchase price under each of four contracts and there were 375 kilograms of unused yarn intact on their premises. The plaintiffs claimed the return of this, but solicitors for the receiver rejected their claim on the ground that the retention of title clause was invalid for non-registration under section 95 of the Companies Act 1948.

The receiver appropriated the yarn and used it in the manufacturing process. The plaintiffs therefore sued him for damages for conversion of their goods.

After an eight day hearing in the Manchester Chancery Court, Judge O'Donoghue, sitting as a deputy judge of the High Court, dismissed the claim. He held that Condition 12 created a charge on the yarn which was void for non-registration under section 95 of the Companies Act 1948, but he did not specify in his lengthy judgment under which sub-section of that section it should have been registered.

In the Court of Appeal counsel for the respondents sought to uphold that finding. Lord Justice Robert Goff in his judgment said:

'It is submitted by counsel for the respondents that, if the first sentence is read literally ... the buyers can only have had possession of the yarn in a fiduciary capacity, whether as bailees or as fiduciary agents. But the power conferred on the Buyers under the contract, not merely to sell the material but also to mix it with other materials in the manufacture of goods, was inconsistent with the existence of any fiduciary capacity in the Buyers, or indeed with the Appellants' unqualified ownership of the yarn. In support of this submission, he [counsel] relied in particular on a proposition derived from the judgment of Slade J in *In re Bond Worth*, when he said:

> "... where an alleged trustee has the right to mix tangible assets or moneys with his own assets or moneys and to deal with them as he pleases, this is incompatible with the existence of a presently subsisting fiduciary relationship in regard to such particular assets or money".'

Lord Justice Robert Goff then said: 'This is a submission which I am unable to accept'. With that the two other judges agreed.

It is now clear that, as was said in the *Romalpa* case, there can be a bailment where the prospective purchaser is entitled to process the goods or sell them on his own behalf as well as being an agent and bailee for the seller.

Lord Justice Robert Goff expressly said:

> 'I can see nothing objectionable in an agreement between parties under which A, the owner of goods, gives possession of those goods to B, at the same time conferring on B a power of sale and a power to consume the goods in manufacture, though A will remain the owner of the goods until they are either sold or consumed. I do not see why the relationship between A and B, pending sale or consumption should not be the relationship of bailor and bailee, even though A has no right to trace the property in his goods into the proceeds of sale. If that is what the parties have agreed should happen, I can see no reason why the law should not give effect to that intention. I am happy to find that both Staughton J and Peter Gibson J have adopted a similar approach in the recently reported cases of *Hendy Lennox (Industrial Engines) Ltd* v. *Grahame Puttick Ltd* (1983).'

On this point, therefore, it can be said without qualification that the judgment of Mr Justice Slade, as he then was, has been conclusively over-ruled.

Also expressly disapproved was the proposition in *In re Bond Worth* which was advanced by Mr Justice Slade as follows:

> 'In my judgment, any contract which, by way of security for payment of a debt, confers an interest in property defeasible or destructible upon

payment of such debt, or appropriates such property for the discharge of the debt, must necessarily be regarded as creating a mortgage or charge, as the case may be. The existence of the equity of redemption is quite inconsistent with the existence of a bare trustee-beneficiary relationship.'

As to that, Lord Justice Robert Goff said:

'So far as the retention of title in unused materials is concerned, I see no difficulty in distinguishing the present case from that envisaged by Slade J. Under the first sentence of the Condition, the Buyer does not, by way of security, confer on the Seller an interest in property defeasible upon the payment of the debt so secured. On the contrary, the Seller retains the legal property in the material.'

Sir John Donaldson MR thought it a simple issue:

'The agreement between the Plaintiffs and the company involved the Plaintiffs retaining property in the goods. It did not involve the company conferring a charge on any property, still less on its own property.'

8.13   Do aggregation clauses constitute a charge?

It was also argued that the aggregation clause created an interest in the seller's property and so must have constituted a charge; and from this counsel argued that the seller's rights in unused materials should likewise be construed as a charge. Lord Justice Robert Goff said:

'It is no doubt true that, where A's material is lawfully used by B to create new goods, whether or not B incorporated other material of his own, property in the new goods will generally vest in B, at least where the goods are not reducible to the original materials: see Blackstone. Comm. 404–5.
  But it is difficult to see why, if the parties agree that the property in the goods shall vest in A, that agreement should not be given effect to.
  On this analysis, under the last sentence of the Condition as under the first, the Buyer does not confer on the Seller an interest in property defeasible upon the payment of the debt; on the contrary, when the new goods come into existence the property in them *ipso facto* vests in the Seller, and he thereafter retains his ownership in them, in the same way

and on the same terms as he retains his ownership in the unused material.'

However, he did conclude that the aggregation clause might constitute a charge:

'Consistent with the approach of Vinelott J to a similar provision in *In Re Peachdart Ltd* (1984), I have come to the conclusion that, *although it does indeed do violence to the language of the fourth sentence of the condition,* that sentence must be read as giving rise to a charge on the new goods in favour of the buyer.'

But he held that:

'Even so, I do not see why the presence of the last sentence in the condition should prevent us from giving effect to the first sentence in accordance with its terms.

The fact that I feel driven to do violence to the language of the last sentence of the condition is not of itself enough to persuade me that further violence must be done to the language of the first.

The provision in the first sentence is perfectly clear. The concept of retention of title – or reservation of the right of disposal – pending payment of the price is, and has for very many years, been well known in commerce, as section 19(1) of the Sale of Goods Act 1979 clearly demonstrates.

For my part I cannot see why, if the law should require that the last sentence, expressed to be a retention of title, must nevertheless take effect as a charge, we should be required to impose a meaning on the first sentence which conflicts with the natural and ordinary meaning of the words there used.'

His lordship, although he held that the aggregation clause might constitute a charge, did not expressly hold that it was a registrable charge; still less did he specify with which of the three categories specified in section 95 of the Companies Act 1948 it fell.

8.14 Simple retention of title clauses cannot constitute a charge

Lord Justice Oliver made the position entirely clear with the words:

'On the face of it therefore, the opening words of clause 12 constitute no more than a simple reservation of the seller's ownership of the goods pending the fulfilment of one or other of the specified conditions.

On this footing no question of any charge by the buyer requiring registration under section 95 of the Companies Act 1948 can arise because a company can create a charge only on its own property and if it never acquires a property in the goods the subject of an agreement for sale it cannot charge them.

It is said that one must have regard to the purpose of the clause. The whole purpose of the clause, it is said, was to give the appellants security for the payment of the purchase price under each contract and it is argued that the corollary of that is that a charge is created by the buyer in favour of the seller.

There appear to me to be two fallacies to this argument.

In the first place, I question the correctness of the assumption that the whole purpose of the clause is to give the seller security for the payment of the purchase price. No doubt that is a part, and an important part of the purpose of the clause, but put in more general terms its purpose is to protect the seller from the insolvency of the buyer in circumstances where the price remains unpaid. Test it in this way. Goods are delivered to the buyer. Before they are paid for the buyer informs the seller that it is hopelessly insolvent, that a liquidator has been appointed and that the seller can no longer have any hope or expectation that the buyer will be able to perform its contract. That is a clear repudiation which the seller can, and clearly will, accept.

He then proceeds to repossess the goods and sells them elsewhere. But he does so not as a mortgagee who must account to the liquidator for any balance over and above the purchase price but as the owner of goods in respect of which no further contractual rights are exercisable by the buyer. If there is a shortfall he may prove in the liquidation for damages for breach of contract. But at no stage after the acceptance of the buyer's repudiation is the liquidator entitled to re-establish the contract and to defeat the seller's proprietary right in the subject matter by tendering the price.

Thus, as it seems to me, the purpose of the clause goes well beyond a mere security for payment of the price.

But secondly, and even assuming that the respondents' basic proposition is correct, the corollary claimed simply does not follow as a necessary or logical consequence.

Of course, where the legal title has passed, security can be provided by a charge created by the new legal owner. But it is not a necessary incident of the seller's securing his position that he should pass the legal title. The whole question is, how has his position been secured. If in fact he has retained the legal title to the goods, then by definition the buyer cannot have charged them in his favour.'

8.15   Contractual provisions regarding an aggregation clause may be effective

In regard to aggregation clauses, Lord Justice Oliver said:

'English law has developed no sophisticated system for determining title in cases where indistinguishable goods are mixed or become combined in a newly manufactured article and to adopt the words of Lord Moulton in *Sandeman & Sons* v. *Tyzack & Brandfoot SS Co.* (1913): "The whole matter is far from being within the domain of settled law". I prefer to reserve my opinion.

I am not sure that I see any reason in principle why the original legal title in a newly manufactured article composed of materials belonging to A and B should not lie where A and B have agreed that it shall lie.'

With respect to his lordship, he is plainly right. Section 17 of the Sale of Goods Act 1979 makes it perfectly clear that contracting parties are entitled to provide when the property of goods is to pass; moreover, at common law, contracting parties are entitled to decide where the ownership of future goods shall rest.

If, therefore, the parties decide that on the admixture of the seller's goods with those of the buyer, title should rest in the seller, it is the duty of the courts to give effect to this contractual arrangement.

8.16   Conclusions from the *Clough Mill* case

This decision of the Court of Appeal makes it plain that if there is an express retention of title clause, the court will give effect to it, even though the purpose of it is to secure payment to the sellers in priority to those who are secured creditors. *In re Bond Worth Ltd* must be regarded as not merely discredited but totally over-ruled.

The case also upheld 'current account' clauses [4.03], but expressly declined to define the effects of an aggregation clause [4.06], although there were *obiter dicta* from two judges to the effect that they could see no reason why the contract of the parties should not be implemented by the courts [7.07]. To that extent, *In re Peachdart Ltd* (1983) and *re Andrabell Ltd* (1984) must now be regarded as dubious authority.

As a matter of law, they are plainly wrong: see [7.01 *et seq.*].

8.17 The Companies Registration Office

At one time, after the *Romalpa* case, the Companies Registration Office refused to register retention of title clauses as company charges. After *In re Bond Worth Ltd*, they agreed to accept them.

The current position is that they accept, after the *Clough Mill* case, that straightforward retention of title clauses are not registrable. However, they apparently adopt the view that 'proceeds of sale' clauses constitute a charge on book debts and are therefore registrable. Furthermore, they take the view that in view of the observations, all *obiter*, of the Court of Appeal in *Clough Mill*, 'aggregation clauses' are registrable, although they are not prepared to specify under which sub-section of section 396 they are registrable.

As they accurately comment:

'Undoubtedly the interpretation of legislation is a matter for the courts and not for either the Registrar of Companies or the Department of Trade and Industry.'

There are three comments that may be made on the present position. Section 399 of the Companies Act 1985 provides:

'399(2)—Where registration is effected upon application of some person other than the company, that person is entitled to recover from the company the amount of any fees properly paid by him to the registrar on the registration.'

It is to be hoped that suppliers who find it necessary to register the alleged charges will recover these sums from their intending purchasers.

Secondly, an application to the Registrar of Companies which is refused is as valid as a registered charge: *N.V. Slavenburg's Bank* v. *Intercontinental* (1981).

Thirdly, it is difficult to see how any supplier of materials can possibly comply with the requirements of Section 401(1)(b) in respect of the Companies Act 1985 in respect of aggregation clauses. They are required to specify

(a) the date of its creation;
(b) when the company creating the charge acquired the property;
(c) the amount secured by the charge;
(d) particulars of the property charged.

However, the Registry apparently takes the view that there would be no difficulties in completing their registration form within twenty-one days after the making of an agreement which constitutes a charge in favour of the seller of materials over goods to be manufactured in future by the producer, being goods which include materials supplied.

Is the 'date of creation' every single invoice recording the delivery of goods subject to these conditions? If so, the populace of Cardiff can expect a rapid diminution of their unemployment figures. If not, what?

When does the company 'subject to the charge' acquire the property? That is, if the retention of title clause specifies that the company shall not become the owner until the supplier has been paid.

If goods are supplied with an aggregation clause which specifies explicitly that admixed materials shall become the property of the suppliers, when does the intending purchaser ever acquire property? And what is the supplier, who disputes that the intending purchaser will even become the owner of admixed goods, expected to inform the Register of Companies about when the intending purchaser 'acquired the property'?

The supplier with a simple retention of title may be able to designate 'the amount secured by the charge' but how can it cover a supplier who has a 'current account' clause – now expressly approved by the Court of Appeal in *Clough Mill*. And when there is an aggregation clause how can a supplier specify particulars of the property to be charged when he has no knowledge of what that property may be or when it may be made?

All this, it will be recalled, has to be filed within twenty-one days of the contract. It is quite apparent that it is impossible for any supplier with an aggregation clause to comply in any way with section 399 and the *obita dicta* of the judges of the Court of Appeal in *Clough Mill* should be regarded as unsound. The Registrar of the Companies Registration Office must surely be well advised to do the same or else run the risk of being personally liable for negligence.

Chapter 9

The Position of Receivers and Administrators

9.01 The receiver and the assets of a company

A receiver appointed by a secured creditor is in a different position entirely from a liquidator of a company. Such powers as this type of receiver possesses are derived not from law but from the instrument, usually a debenture, which regulates the position of the company and the secured creditors. The assets of the company do not vest in the receiver, although he has the power to realise them by sale. He does not become a party to contracts in existence with the company, and it follows that he cannot vary such contracts.

In *Parsons* v. *Sovereign Bank of Canada* (1912), Parsons were merchants who had contracts for the supply of paper over three years with the Imperial Paper Mills Ltd. When those contracts had still two years to run, a receiver with power to manage Imperial Paper Mills was appointed by the court at the instance of Sovereign Bank who held debentures in the company. The receiver purported to cancel the contracts at the time when Parsons owed $15,754 to the company. Parsons therefore deducted, by way of set-off from this sum, damages for breach of contract. Discussing the appointment of a receiver, Lord Haldane said:

'The company remains in existence, but has lost its title to control its assets and its affairs . . .

In the absence of a liquidation, the persona of the . . . company remains legally intact though controlled by the receivers and managers . . .

In the case of contracts to deliver paper . . . there appears to be no reason for saying that the possession of the undertaking and the assets [by the receivers] . . . put an end to these contracts. The company [Imperial Paper Mills] remained in legal existence and so did the contracts until put an end to otherwise.'

The court, therefore, held that the company, and therefore its assignees, the bank, could not sue for the price of paper delivered to Parsons except subject to Parsons' counter-claim for damages. As these exceeded the amount of the claim, nothing was due to the company's assignees, the bank.

So, too, in *George Barker (Transport) Ltd* v. *Eynon* (1974), Lord Justice Edmund Davis, as he then was, said of the appointment of a receiver:

'He must fulfil company trading contracts entered into before his appointment or he renders it liable in damages if he unwarrantably declines to do so: see the authorities conveniently collected in *Buckley on the Companies Acts*, 13th Edition (1957), page 244.

Neither the receiver nor the debenture holders were in any way relieved by the former's appointment from the obligations which, by pre-appointment contracts, the company had undertaken.'

Consequently, the Court of Appeal held that the plaintiffs, a transport firm carrying meat for the company concerned, were entitled to a contractual lien over the goods carried, even after the appointment of the receiver.

Two things necessarily follow from this position of a receiver:

(1) If the receiver takes possession of the assets of a company and he finds in possession of the company goods which remain, as the result of a retention of title clause, the property of the unpaid seller, he is subject to exactly the same contractual conditions as was the company. There can be no question of the debenture holders having any rights which rank in priority to those of the unpaid seller.

(2) The receiver can only acquire title to the goods in exactly the same way the company can, i.e. by paying the full amount due to the seller.

It follows that a legal retention of title clause, which authorises the company to sell on the goods and receives the rights to the proceeds of resale to the seller, is effective against a receiver and debenture holders.

9.02 Personal liability of a receiver

In circumstances where a company resells goods subject to a retention of title clause without the express or implied authority of the owners, the owners may claim damages for conversion of the goods, which damages will be quantified in accordance with the principles set out in the Torts

(Interference with Goods) Act 1977. In essence, the damages will normally be not the price at which the seller would be prepared to sell to the intending buyer but the damages suffered by the wrongful disposal.

In the event of a liquidation of a company, such damages will, when quantified by a court, rank only with the claims of unsecured creditors. Moreover, claims for damages for a tort, as distinct from claims for damages for breach of contract, are excluded from proof in a liquidation, until quantified by judgment.

But in the event of an unauthorised sale by a receiver, he will be personally liable to the owner for the damages.

Two situations may arise: where the receiver sells the goods without knowing of the retention of title clause, and where he knows of the retention clause. In the first case he will be personally liable for damages for conversion, but will be entitled to an indemnity out of the company's assets in priority to the claims of the debenture holders: *Scott* v. *Nesbitt* (1808); *In re Rylands Glass Co.* (1904).

Where the receiver knows of the retention of title clause and yet sells the goods, it would appear that he will be liable for damages for conversion without right of recourse to the funds of the company. It is immaterial that he thinks the retention clause is not valid, even if he has cause.

This will apply even where he purports to vest the property of the goods in a 'hive-down' company. The goods are not the property of the company to which the receiver has been appointed. The proceedings for damages should be launched against the receiver personally and not against the company in receivership since it is not a tort by the company; and even if damages were recovered against the company, they would only rank after judgment with unsecured creditors and are therefore likely to be irrecoverable in the usual circumstances of a liquidation.

If the receiver has paid to the debenture holders the proceeds of the sale of the goods which were not the company's to sell, he may well not be able to recover from them such monies, because these are monies paid under a mistake of law rather than fact. But in any event the damages and costs for which he will have to become liable will inevitably exceed the price at which he has sold off the goods.

However, whether the unauthorised sale is by the company or its receiver, the vendor with a retention clause will also be able to claim that the company is bailee of the goods and therefore in a fiduciary position. Thereby, he can hold the company or its receiver liable to account for the value of the goods under the tracing principles set out in *In re Hallett's Estate* (1880), and exemplified in the *Romalpa* case itself. If the proceeds of sale can be traced into the company on the receiver's account, the full amount can be recovered. If the price has not been paid by the sub-purchaser, the unpaid vendor can recover it directly from him.

9.03 Receivers and registration of charges

Section 95 of the Companies Act 1948 and section 395 and 396 of the Companies Act 1985 [8.02] make unregistered charges void only against 'the liquidator and any creditor of the company'.

A receiver appointed by a debenture holder, such as a bank, is neither a 'liquidator nor a creditor'. He is not even the authorised agent of a creditor since all debenture forms in current use are careful to specify that he shall be solely the agent of the company to which he is appointed and not the agent of the secured creditor who appoints him: and the Insolvency Act 1985 confirms this position [9.04].

As such he is bound by all contracts of the company [9.01] and by all charges of the company whether registered or not registered, and is estopped from raising assertions which the company would be estopped from raising. His powers are no greater than those of the company to whom he is appointed.

Admittedly under section 369 of the Companies Act 1948, now incorporated in slightly different words in section 492 of the Companies Act 1985, he is entitled to apply to the court in wide terms in relation to any particular matters arising in connection with the performance of his functions.

The exact wording is:

Section 492 (1). A receiver or manager of the property of a company appointed under powers contained in an instrument may apply to the court for directions in relation to any particular matter arising in connection with the performance of his functions.

Section 492 (2). On such an application, the court may give such directions, or may make such order, declaring the rights of persons before the court or otherwise, as it thinks just.

It has not yet been raised in any court that 'the performance of his functions' does not include determining whether a particular retention of title clause constitutes a charge that is void as against 'a liquidator or any creditor'. He is not the agent of any creditor; he is solely and exclusively the agent of the company. As such he is bound by all the contractual relationships into which the company has entered and is estopped from denying the validity of any of its transactions.

Had objection been taken in proper form in *In re Bond Worth Ltd, In re Peachdart Ltd, re Andrabell Ltd,* the receivers would have been sent away with a flea in their ear. None had any right to have their applications entertained by the court since none of them related to 'performance of their functions'. Their duty and their functions were to give effect to the contracts and obligations entered into by the companies to which they were appointed receivers.

It is sincerely to be hoped that somebody somewhere will take steps to cut receivers down to size.

The receiver as agent of the company can have no better cause of action than the company has. In *Independent Automatic Sales Ltd* v. *Knowles & Foster* (1963) Mr Justice Buckley was called upon to decide whether a company could itself object that a charge it had itself created and was under a duty by statute to register, had not been registered and was therefore void.

He said:

'What I have to consider is whether the company itself can have any good cause of action arising out of the non-registration of a charge registrable under section 95 of the Act of 1948, and I think the answer to that question is in the negative.

The charge is not made void as against the company; the charge is only made void as against the liquidator and as against creditors of the company.

It seems to me that the rights of the company are wholly unaffected by the section, and consequently, I think on that ground the company is not a proper party to assert that the charge is void for lack of registration.

Moreover . . . section 96 of the Act of 1948 imposes upon the company a statutory duty to register any registrable charge; and consequently *ex hypothesi* – where a charge has not been registered, the company is in default of that statutory obligation, and in an action directed to avoiding such charge for non-registration must necessarily plead its own default.

That is a position which, it seems to me, the company ought not to be allowed to take up, and it reinforces the view which I have reached, on consideration of section 95, that in fact the company is not a proper party to make any such assertion.'

9.04 'Administrative receivers' under the Insolvency Act 1985

The position of receivers appointed by secured creditors is extensively provided for by Part II of the Insolvency Act 1985, in which the new expression 'administrative receiver' appears.

An 'administrative receiver' is defined by section 45(2) of that Act as:

(a) 'a receiver or manager of the whole (or substantially the whole) of a company's property appointed by or on behalf of the holders of any debenture of the company secured by a charge which, as created, was a floating charge and one or more other securities; or

(b) a person who would be such a receiver or manager but for the appointment of some other person as part of the receiver of part of the company's property.'

It will be seen, therefore, that a receiver appointed by, say, a mortgagee or a bank with a fixed charge over certain of a company's assets is excluded from this definition. Extensive powers are conferred upon 'administrative receivers' by Schedule 3 but these are limited to dealings with the company's own property and do not extend to dealings with goods where the supplier has retained title.

The same Act creates a new category of 'administrator' [9.13] to be appointed by the court. By contrast, as will be seen, an 'administrator' has power [9.13] to dispose of goods which are not the company's property. Chapter III of the Insolvency Act 1985 which deals with 'Administrative Orders' is a rather feeble attempt to emulate Chapter 11 of the US Federal legislation for companies. It gives the administrator greater powers than an 'administrative receiver' would have if there is some prospect of ensuring the survival of the company or securing a more advantageous realisation of its assets.

For present purposes, it is worthy of note that the Insolvency Act 1985 specifically provides, in section 50, that

'(1) The administrative receiver of a company
(a) shall be deemed to be the agent of the company unless and until the company goes into liquidation.'

This appears to give statutory effect to the common law position that a receiver is no more than the agent of the company and bound by all the company's contracts and obligations. However, it also seems to preclude the receiver being appointed as agent of the secured creditor, if the debenture, or other document which created the right to appoint a receiver, so provided.

Two things seem to flow from this statutory provision:

(a) The 'administrative receiver' is for all purposes, irrespective of the terms of this appointment, solely the agent of the company.

(b) As such, he is precluded from raising against the company the contention that a retention of title clause constitutes an unregistered charge [9.03] under section 395 or 396 of the Companies Act 1985.

The same section also provides that the 'administrative receiver' shall be 'personally liable on any contract entered into by him in carrying out of his functions'.

These are ambiguous words and they may confirm the position that the receiver who sells goods belonging to another, because they are subject to a retention of title clause, is subject to damages in tort for conversion.

However, it would appear that this statutory liability applies only to '*any contract* entered into by him', and the words should be given their plain meaning. If he purports to sell goods subject to a retention of title clause and the buyer gets no title, he will plainly be liable under this sub-section to the buyer. But, so far as liability to the real owner is concerned, the seller who has retained title has to sue the receiver in tort.

The importance of this is that a receiver is, under section 50(1)(c) of the Act, entitled to an indemnity out of the assets of the company for his personal liability; but this only applies to contracts he has entered into.

It would not apply to the receiver in the *Clough Mill* case who had committed, the Court of Appeal held, the tort of conversion. His costs and the damages awarded against him were recoverable neither from the company nor from those who appointed him (although no doubt as a matter of policy they did meet them).

The Insolvency Act 1985 does not therefore change this position. Receivers are personally liable if they make use of other persons' goods for their own purposes.

9.05 Terms of the contract?

The receiver's first ploy is always to allege that the reservation of title clause is not a term of the contract of sale.

Before a retention of title clause can have any effect it must be a term of the contract of sale. In all the leading English cases mentioned so far, there was a dispute as to whether or not the retention clause was included as a term of the contract.

The plaintiffs in the *Romalpa* case, Aluminium Industrie Vaassen (A.I.V.) alleged that the clause was a term of the contract with Romalpa Ltd, either expressly or impliedly. The defendants admitted that it did apply to trade that had been carried on previously between A.I.V. and a partnership called Romalpa Aluminium, prior to the plaintiffs beginning to do business with the limited company Romalpa Aluminium Ltd on 1st September 1979, but contended that the clause did not apply to dealings with A.I.V. thereafter.

Mr Justice Mocatta, the trial judge, having considered the facts, concluded that the general selling terms and conditions as applied to the dealings between A.I.V. and the partnership Romalpa Aluminium, also applied to dealings between the plaintiffs and the defendants. There is no published report of his findings on the issue, but in the Court of Appeal, Lord Justice Roskill adverted to the circumstances of the incorporation by reference:

'The plaintiffs did their business on certain general conditions of sale dated February 1971 which were deposited or registered with all district or county courts in Holland . . . Those conditions were in Dutch, but there was what one might describe as an authentic and specially prepared, though not very well expressed, English translation of the Dutch conditions. On 4 April 1972, the plantiffs obtained from the partnership (Romalpa Aluminium), the signature of the two partners on a copy of that English translation. The conditions were expressed to be subject to Dutch law, the Amsterdam court being given exclusive jurisdiction . . .'

Later, said his lordship, the company took over the business carried on by the partnership and continued to do business on those terms.

'Individual invoices covering specific transactions incorporated both in Dutch and English what was described as 'an epitome' of the plaintiffs' general conditions . . . One hesitates to criticise such a document, for one knows the difficulties of translation of this type of document from one language to another; but it cannot be said that the English translation is happy.

   Clause 13 (the retention of title clause) is not referred to in the epitome at all – an omission on which the defendants placed considerable reliance in connection with their submission that, though the general conditions had governed the relationship of the plaintiffs with the partnership, they never governed the plaintiffs' relationship with the defendants, notwithstanding that exactly the same printed form of invoice was used . . .'

Lord Justice Roskill then adopted the findings of fact made by Mr Justice Mocatta:

'The full deposited terms, including clause 13, did apply to every order placed by the defendants with the plaintiffs. I say that, firstly, because the acknowledged form referred at the front to the epitome behind and clause 13 was in fact part of the general selling terms and conditions filed with the Dutch county courts . . . Secondly, if there were any doubts on this point, I would have no hesitation in holding that the full terms, including clause 13, were impliedly agreed to apply to each order.'

In the judgment of Lord Justice Megaw, he describes the documents in existence. An Acknowledgement of Order bore on its face the words 'Vide epitome of our General Selling Terms at the back'. The so-called epitome on the back, which included no reference to the retention of title clause 13, purported to describe the 'General Selling Terms and Conditions . . . which general selling terms and conditions are filed at the Record Office of all County Courts in the Netherlands'.

It is not proposed in this book to comment on those findings of the trial judge and the Court of Appeal. It is sufficient to say that the company, because of previous transactions by the partnership from which it had acquired the business, and because of the actual admitted knowledge of the directors, was saddled with the vital clause 13 as a term of the conditions of sale.

The courts did not decide that to print on the face of an Acknowledgement of Order a reference to an epitome on the back of terms deposited in Dutch in some local courts in the Netherlands was sufficient notice as to incorporate those terms into the contract. In fact, Lord Justice Megaw said that he did not resile from the observations he had made in *Thornton* v. *Shoe Lane Parking Ltd* (1971):

'Where the particular condition relied upon involves a sort of restriction that is not shown to be usual in that class of contract, a defendant must show that his intention to attach an unusual condition of that particular nature was fairly brought to the notice of the other party.'

Retention of title clauses will not be implied, and had the transactions between A.I.V. and Romalpa Ltd taken place between parties coming afresh to do business with no antecedent transactions between them, it is most unlikely that the vital clause 13 would have been held to be a term of the contract of sale.

The fact that the buyer knows that there are conditions imposed by the seller is not notice of the contents of those conditions: *British Crane Hire* v. *Ipswich Plant Hire* (1975).

The procedure for ordering the Acrilan used for the manufacture of carpets in the *Bond Worth* case was described thus by the trial judge:

'Bond Worth's orders were submitted in writing on printed order forms . . . They were then acknowledged by Monsanto in writing on a series of printed confirmation notes, but on a piecemeal basis, so that each confirmation note would relate to less than the full quantity ordered and, correspondingly, two or more confirmation notes would have to be sent before the full quantity was covered. It appears that each confirmation note was accompanied by a set of Monsanto's standard conditions of sale . . .

Paragraph 10 of the conditions of sale read as follows:

"This contract constitutes the full understanding of the parties and a full and exclusive statement of the terms of their agreement. Except as provided in Section 1 hereof, no conditions, understanding or agreement purporting to modify or vary the terms of this contract shall be binding unless made in writing and signed by the party to be bound and no modifications shall be effected by the acknowledgement or acceptance of the purchase orders or shipment instructions containing terms or conditions at variance or in addition to those set forth . . ."

The conditions of sale, however, contained no provision expressly reserving to Monsanto any legal or beneficial property or interest in the goods pending payment of the full purchase price.'

His lordship held on the facts that each of the 29 contracts with which he was concerned were not concluded by the acceptance of the order placed by Bond Worth by the issue of a confirmation note by Monsanto, but when the goods in question were actually delivered to and accepted by Bond Worth.

On 30 June 1976, Monsanto wrote a letter to Bond Worth:

'Dear Sirs,

Change in conditions of sale

Would you please note that with effect from July 1st 1976 we are amending our standard terms of contract insofar as all future business will be conducted on normal terms and conditions of sale, except that the following clause shall be incorporated into any contract to the exclusion of any conflicting provisions in our standard terms as presently appears on our confirmation or orders.

(a) The risk in the goods passes to the buyer upon delivery, but equitable and beneficial ownership shall remain with us until full payment has been received, (each order being considered as a

whole), or until prior resale, in which case our beneficial entitlement shall attach to the proceeds of resale or to the claim for such
proceeds.

(b) Should the goods become constituents of or be converted into other
products while subject to our equitable and beneficial ownership
we shall have the equitable and beneficial ownership in such other
products as if they were solely and simply the goods and
accordingly sub-clause (a) shall as appropriate apply to such other
products.

We would appreciate your acknowledgement that this clause now
applies to future deliveries to your good selves by signing the attached
copy letter and returning it to us.'

The company secretary of Bond Worth signed the copy and returned it to
Monsanto.

Notwithstanding that letter, Monsanto continued to issue, with their
confirmation notes, conditions of sale which made no reference to these
terms and in fact prohibited any alteration from the terms printed. Was
the retention clause contained in the letter a term of the contract of sale in
these circumstances?

His lordship made a finding of fact:

'So long as Bond Worth remained apparently good for the money, the
retention of title clause seems for practical purposes to have been
forgotten by both the interested parties.'

His conclusion, therefore, was by no means inevitable. He said:

'On the face of it, two points seem to me clear in relation to this
correspondence. First, Monsanto thereby proposed and Bond Worth
thereby agreed that notwithstanding any conflicting provisions appear-
ing in Monsanto's printed standard conditions of sale (such as condition
10 in particular) the retention of title clause should be deemed to be
incorporated in any future contract for the sale and purchase of any
goods which might thereafter be delivered by Monsanto to Bond
Worth.

Secondly, both parties must be taken to have intended that the
agreement thus concluded should have legal effect.

In these circumstances my initial reaction to this correspondence is
to give effect to the agreement embodied in it, unless there is some
compelling reason to the contrary.'

That conclusion does not appear to be supported by the letter itself. That announced a future intention to amend the standard terms of contract '. . . with effect from July 1st 1976, we are amending our standard terms of contract . . .' No such amendment took place and, on the judge's own findings, the parties forgot all about the letter.

Another judge might well on those facts have concluded that the retention of title terms formed no part of the contract of sale since the offer was made by the issue of a confirmation note to which was attached the unamended conditions of sale, purporting to be as inviolable as the law of the Medes and Persians, and the acceptance was by the act of receiving delivery of goods, and each delivery constituted a separate contract.

9.06 The battle of the forms

These two cases illustrate how narrowly the retention of title clause was held to be part of the contract of sale. Such disputes are likely to be common since what frequently happens is:

Round one: Intending buyer asks for quotation on his printed form which contains the terms on which the buyer is willing to do business.
Round two: Intending supplier quotes on his own printed terms and conditions of supply, which include a retention of title clause.
Round three: Buyer places an order on his own printed order form which, *inter alia*, rejects the inclusion of any retention of title clause, usually by stating that the terms set out in the buyer's order form alone shall govern the contract.
Round four: goods are supplied with a delivery note repeating the supplier's terms and conditions, including the retention of title clause. The buyer's gateman signs for the goods and takes them into stock.

The question is, is there a contract for the sale of goods and, if so, on what terms?

On basic principles, the answer may well be that there is no contract of any kind. Traditionally, unless the parties are agreed as to all essential terms, there is no contract. That, at least, is what students are taught in accordance with the cases of *Hyde* v. *Wrench* (1840); *Neale* v. *Merrett* (1930); *Northland Airlines Ltd* v. *Dennis Ferranti Meters Ltd* (1970) etc.

The learned editor of *Cheshire and Fifoot on The Law of Contract* (9th Edition, page 151) appears to support this view, while conceding that in practice the courts will not adopt it but try to give some commercial effect to what the parties have done. The learned editor of *Anson on Contract*

(24th Edition, page 37), however, supports the view that there should be held to be a binding contract in spite of the old rules.

It should also be borne in mind that if goods are in fact supplied, but on the facts that there is no express contract, the courts may imply a quasi-contractual obligation on the buyer to pay for goods received on the basis of a *quantum valebant* (i.e. the market value of the goods, which may not be the agreed price) and in that case the transaction will not incorporate any term about retention of title. (See also section 8(2) of the Sale of Goods Act 1979).

Excluding no 'express contract' and 'no implied contract' as answers to the problem, if there is a contract is it on (a) the seller's terms or (b) the buyer's terms?

In general the courts in England have inclined to the view that the winner of the battle of the forms is 'the last past the post'. In other words, if goods are accepted by the buyers on certain conditions put forward by the seller, those conditions apply.

Those were the findings of the court in *British Road Services Ltd* v. *Arthur* v. *Crutchley & Co. Ltd* (1968) where, however, there had been previous dealings between the parties. A load of whisky was delivered by British Road Services to a warehouse belonging to the defendants who stamped the plaintiff's delivery note 'Received on A.V.C.'s Conditions'. The whisky was stolen while in the defendants' possession. On whose conditions were the goods stored: on those contained in the plaintiff's printed delivery note or on the defendants' condition annexed by the rubber stamped words? Needless to say, the conditions were entirely incompatible. The Court of Appeal held that the defendants' conditions were incorporated in their contract with the plaintiffs by reason of the rubber stamp. But had the lorry driver power or authority to bind his employers?

In the later case of *Butler Machine Tool Co. Ltd* v. *Ex-Cell-O Corporation (England) Ltd* (1979) the court again opted for the 'last past the post' solution. The following sequence of events had taken place:

Round one: The plaintiffs offered a machine tool to the defendants on terms containing a price fluctuation clause.
Round two: The defendants accepted the offer on their own standard order form, which had no price fluctuation clause, but which had a tear-off form which read: 'We accept your order on the Terms and Conditions stated thereon'.
Round three: The plaintiffs completed and returned this slip to the defendants.
Round four: The plaintiffs supplied the machine tool without imposing other terms on their delivery note.

Later, the plaintiffs sought to claim an escalation of the price under their price fluctuation clause. The Court of Appeal held that the goods had been bought on the buyers' (the defendants') terms and those terms contained no provisions for escalation.

It is therefore most important that suppliers of goods should when they quote a price make it plain that the goods will only be supplied on their terms. To include terms as to retention of title on an invoice is far too late. The terms must be imposed before the contract is made.

If the offer to supply goods is made on the suppliers' standard terms which include a retention of title clause, and an acceptance is received on the buyers' standard terms which exclude a retention of title clause and make provisions inconsistent with the sellers' terms, then this constitutes not an acceptance of the offer but a counter-offer. If goods are then supplied without any further contact between the parties, they will be on the buyers' terms, since the supply will be deemed to be 'an acceptance *by conduct*' of the buyers' counter-offer.

Where orders are placed on the buyers' terms, the supplier has two options to preserve his rights. He can either refuse the order, which no doubt he will be reluctant to do; or he can send a written 'Confirmation of Order' which says politely:

'We thank you for your esteemed order which we note purports to be on terms incompatible with our standard conditions of sale, a copy of which we once more draw to your attention. We propose to fulfil your order on our standard terms unless we hear from you to the contrary within seven days and on terms that acceptance of the goods by you or your staff or carriers on your behalf shall be deemed to be acceptance of our goods on our terms.'

The delivery note should make it plain that the goods are supplied on the supplier's standard terms as previously disclosed to the buyers.

9.07 Ensuring that retention of title clauses are a term of the contract

From this, it is clear that it is of paramount importance to ensure that a retention of title clause is in fact a term of the contract of sale.

To print it on the back of an invoice is far too late: the contract of sale has been made much earlier. It may be effective where there are continuing transactions between the parties so that a court can infer that these terms had been accepted. But in the case of first orders, it is essential that the supplier should with his offer of the goods specify in detail the terms on which they are offered; and that any orders placed on inconsistent terms are rejected.

Companies are appallingly lax in ensuring that the terms upon which goods are sold are clear. As a result they often find themselves deprived of payment and, even worse, involved in litigation. Receivers are experts in exploiting this situation.

9.08 Identification of the goods

The second ploy of the receiver is to claim that the goods on hand cannot be identified. In particular, the receiver will question whether the particular goods on the premises were actually supplied by the supplier. This is often a difficult question, particularly for the construction industry. One load of bricks normally cannot be identified from another, nor can sanitary ware and pipes. In fact, most building materials cannot be identified against specific invoices.

One solution of this problem is for the supplier who has retained title to use strong-arm tactics to repossess the goods. In one case known to the present writer, the supplier had sent a load of bricks to a building site on a Friday morning; in the afternoon of that day, a receiver appointed by a bank took possession of the site and the contractor's business. The receiver refused to acknowledge that the delivery of bricks could be identified as the supplier's property even though they were supplied on terms that (a) the property should not pass until payment and (b) the suppliers should have a right to entry of the property to repossess them.

The following Sunday morning, the supplier sent a lorry to the site, cut the wire, loaded his bricks on to lorries and took them away. He resealed the wire and advised the police what he had done. Neither the police nor the receiver took any action. To start with, the suppliers were not trespassers since they had in their contract an express right to enter the premises. They were not guilty of theft because they genuinely believed they were repossessing their own goods, as indeed they were.

It is suggested by receivers that the onus of proof rests upon the supplier to prove that his goods are in the possession of the receiver. Possession, it is said, is nine tenths of the law.

However, it is certain once goods have been repossessed that the onus rests on the receiver to prove that he has title to them. This is a task that he will be most unwilling to undertake, not least of all because of the liability to pay costs in the event of failure. There is good reason therefore why those who have goods on the premises of a company to which a receiver has been appointed should take effective directions to respossess their goods, including those processed into other goods.

It is common for receivers to raise other questions about the identification of goods. Were the goods although manufactured by the claimants actually supplied by another supplier? Which goods related to any particular invoice?

It is therefore most important that the suppliers of goods subject to a retention of title clause should, wherever possible, identify by serial numbers the actual goods supplied under an invoice.

9.09 Injunctions against receivers

At an early stage it is important that a supplier with a retention of title clause who does not wish to exercise his direct rights of self-help against a company should obtain an injunction against the receiver. This can be obtained *ex parte* and prevents the receiver from disposing of the supplier's goods pending the trial. Invariably the receiver will seek to avoid such a clause by inviting the supplier to consent to the disposal of the goods in return for an undertaking that the proceeds thereof will be deposited in a separate bank account, possibly in the name of the joint solicitors, pending resolution of the dispute.

This is a course which cannot be commended to a supplier who has a retention of title clause, even though most solicitors may recommend this course. It is tactically inadvisable since it allows the receiver to deal with the goods as if the company was the owner and leaves the supplier with the difficult task of rebutting an application to the court by a receiver under section 492(1) of the Companies Act 1985. On such an application, the supplier has no right in law to be represented and such applications come before the Chancery Division of the High Court where the court appears to favour moneylenders.

9.10 The presumption of legitimacy

Where part of a supplier's goods has been utilised by the prospective purchaser and some has been paid for and some has not, it is common for the receiver to claim that those on hand in his possession are those paid for, in which case title has passed to the company. This places the burden of proof on the supplier to establish that the goods in the hands of the receiver have not been paid for – by no means an easy task.

However, this is quite contrary to law and equity. There is a presumption both at common law and in chancery, that a prospective purchaser has used his own goods first before those of another. This springs from the Latin tag *omnia praesumuntur rite et solemniter esse acta* – 'There is a presumption that all acts have been rightly and correctly performed'. An honest tradesman will use his own goods before using those of another. This is another aspect of the rule which was applied in *In re Hallett's* case mentioned earlier in the *Romalpa* case [5.03].

Hallett's solicitor had a bank account in which he mingled his own personal money, money subject to a formal trust and client's monies which were subject to an implied trust. He died. The funds on the account were insufficient to meet his personal liabilities and the trust monies and the client's. It was held that whatever sums he had withdrawn from his bank account, it must be presumed to have been his own monies and therefore the balance must first be assigned to the trust monies and client's monies.

The rule is similar so far as goods are concerned.

9.11 Voidable title of goods

Even where there is no express reservation of title, a supplier who has passed a title to a buyer and has not been paid may be entitled to recover the goods if the contract or the possession by the buyer is induced by deceit. The title to the goods is therefore voidable by the seller. It is wise, therefore, to include in conditions of sale an express representation by the prospective purchaser that the company is solvent and knows of no reason why any secured creditor should be entitled to appoint a receiver. If the retention of title clause should by any chance fail to be effective, the transaction can be avoided and the goods repossessed. But if the goods have been sold on before the title has been avoided, a buyer who acquires them in good faith and without notice of his seller's defective title acquires a good title: section 23, Sale of Goods Act 1979. A receiver, of course, is in no better position than the company to resist claims for the repossession of goods sold under a voidable title.

9.12 The Cork Report and retention clauses

Insolvency Law and Practice, the report of the Review Committee presided over by Sir Kenneth Cork and published in 1982, devoted a whole chapter to the subject of 'Reservation of Title'. It had been urged by many of those who gave evidence before it that it should produce an interim report on the subject because the topic was important and urgent.

It was urged on the Committee that proliferation of retention of title clauses would strike at the roots of systems of credit, in that banks would be less able to lend, and factoring of book debts would cease. It was urged on them that receivers would have difficulties in keeping businesses going if stock, work in progress and debtors could be seized by supply creditors. It was pointed out that while the supplier of goods could protect himself by a reservation of title clause, no similar protection was available to the supplier of consumables or services.

> 'Fuel supplied to heat furnaces or fodder supplied for livestock disappears on consumption and paint applied to the fabric of a factory becomes attached to the realty.'

These suggestions were directed to inviting the Committee to suggest that all reservation of title clauses should be made void in insolvency. But the Committee rejected this suggestion.

> 'It would be anomalous of us to countenance the continuation of security in its ordinary form of fixed or floating charge but to deny the continuation of the quasi-security of the reservation of title clause.'

They conceded that the principal beneficiaries would be secured creditors:

> 'Suppliers have opted for reservation of title clauses precisely because they seek to avoid the unfairness which results when they supply goods on credit, a floating charge crystallises, and a receiver then takes the goods and realises them for the benefit of the debenture holder leaving the supplier with nothing.
>
> It seems to us that suppliers are entitled, in such circumstances, to take steps to protect themselves and that it would be wrong to deny them the protection they seek.'

The Committee, however, thought that there was a case for some registration:

> 'The difficulty in requiring disclosure of the use of reservation of title causes flows from the multitude of transactions involved. Clearly it would be a physical impossibility for a register to be kept recording the use of a reservation of title clause in every contract for the sale of goods. We believe, however, that the difficulties of registration can be exaggerated. The essence of the matter is that there should be shown against the name of the *purchaser* first the name of the supplier

imposing reservation of title, secondly a generic description of the types or classes of goods being and to be supplied, and thirdly the maximum amount which at any one time can be secured by the reservation of title. Article 9 of the Uniform Commercial Code of the United States of America has introduced in all the States of the United States, with the exception of Louisiana, the practice of notice filing, which in our view could be adopted and tailored for use in this country and forms a helpful precedent.'

The Committee, however, concluded:

'We have unhesitatingly concluded that it is a small penalty on those who have taken the benefit of reservation of title clauses for their rights to be qualified by a moratorium of up to a year. Accordingly, we recommend:

(a) During a period of 12 months from the commencement of a receivership or an administration a seller should be prevented from exercising rights and remedies flowing from a reservation of title clause in a contract for the sale of goods and a receiver or administrator should be allowed to deal with the goods in a manner *inconsistent* with the title of the supplier.
(b) If the receiver or administrator sells the goods he should be obliged to account to the supplier for the proceeds of sale up to the amount secured by the reservation clause.
(c) If the receiver or administrator uses the goods in the manufacture of some product the proceeds of sale of the product should be applied in or towards the repayment of sums secured on reservation of title clauses *affecting any of the constituent parts of that product*.
(d) In the event of the proceeds being insufficient to pay all suppliers of goods under reservation of title clauses, the claim of each supplier should *abate proportionately* to the respective costs to the company of acquiring the goods incorporated in the product.

In our view, the law would in these circumstances have to permit a supplier from whom a receiver or administrator was withholding goods in which he had an interest under a valid and enforceable reservation of title clause, to seek relief from the Court on the grounds that the moratorium was, in his case, unjust and inequitable: for instance, because
(i) where a sale on of goods in the form in which they were supplied was envisaged, the market was falling, or

(ii) there was no prospect of the manufacture of products incorporating the goods supplied and the sale of those products within the period of one year.'

The Government did not adopt these recommendations of the Cork Committee regarding retention of title clauses when it prepared the Bill which became the Insolvency Act 1985. Indeed, it seemed in two minds what the Act should include, since 1172 amendments to the Bill were tabled in the course of its progress through the two Houses of Parliament.

Receivers, as has been seen [9.04], although they have been rechristened 'administrative receivers', have no power to deal with other people's property which are subject to retention of title clauses. A new animal termed an 'administrator' has, however, power to do so.

9.13 Presentation of a petition for an 'administrator' under the Insolvency Act 1985

An 'administrative receiver' can, as before, be appointed by any secured creditor who has a debenture or a floating charge over the company's assets. An *administrator* can only be appointed by the court and then only if certain conditions are fulfilled.

Firstly, the court has to be satisfied that the company is or is likely to become unable to pay its debts. Secondly, the court has to be satisfied that the appointment of an administrator would be likely to achieve the survival of the company or any part of it as a going concern or a composition, or compromise, with the creditors or 'a more advantageous realisation of the company's assets than would be effected on a winding-up': section 27(3).

The company itself, or its directors, or its creditors can present a petition to the court for the appointment of an administrator. The mere presentation of a petition for the appointment of an 'administrator' brings the shutters down on many forms of action against the company. No proceedings can be commenced (or continued) against the company; no distress can be levied against the company; no order for winding-up can be made and no step can be taken to enforce any security over the company's property.

There is also a very material provision. Section 29(1)(b) provides that:

'no steps may be taken . . . to repossess goods in the company's possession under any hire purchase agreement except with the leave of the court and subject to such terms as the court may impose.'

All that may seem innocuous and unrelated to retention of title clauses. But, unfortunately, section 29(4) of the Act goes on to define 'hire purchase agreements' as including retention of title agreements (and conditional sale agreements and chattel leasing agreements). Section 108(3) defines a retention of title clause as:

'an agreement for the sale of goods to a company, being an agreement – (a) which does not constitute a charge on the goods; but (b) under which, if the seller is not paid and the company is wound up, the seller will have priority over all other creditors of the company as respects the goods or any property representing the goods.'

It is singularly inept definition for goods which remain the seller's property.

However, the effect is this: if the company (or the directors or any creditor) presents a petition for the appointment of an administrator, the presentation of the petition alone is enough to stop the owner of goods subject to a retention of title clause from repossessing his goods – without going to the court and getting leave to do so, or suing for the cost of them.

9.14 After the appointment of an 'administrator'

The court is, as has been indicated earlier, not bound to appoint an administrator and cannot do so unless it is satisfied that certain conditions contained in section 27 of the Insolvency Act 1985 are fulfilled. However, once the court has appointed an administrator, he becomes for all purposes 'deemed to be acting as agent of the company'. He has extensive powers, including that of removing and appointing directors: section 32(2). On his appointment, if an 'administrative receiver' has been approved by a secured creditor, he shall 'vacate office' and no future one can be appointed. Any petition for the winding up of the company shall be dismissed and no steps taken to enforce any security on the company's property.

As in the period between the presentation of the petition and the appointment [9.13], section 30(3)(c) provides:

'no other steps may be taken . . . to repossess goods in the company's possession under any hire purchase agreement.'

But this time the administrator is empowered to consent and the court can also give leave subject to conditions. No other proceedings can be instituted against the company.

Once again, a 'hire purchase' agreement includes a retention of title clause: section 34(12). The 'administrator' is given power to sell other people's goods – subject to an order from the court. Section 34(2) provides:

'Where, on an application by the administrator of a company, the court is satisfied that the disposal . . . of
(b) any goods in the possession of the company under a hire purchase agreement would be likely to promote the purpose . . . specified in the administrator order, the court may by order, authorise the administrator to dispose of the property . . . as if all the rights of the owner under the hire purchase agreement were vested in the company.'

In other words, the 'administrator' is authorised to sell, with the authority of the court, goods in the company's possession which it does not own.

On the face of it, this may seem highly detrimental to a supplier of goods subject to a retention of title clause where an administrator proposes to sell or use them. However, it may possibly be an advantage to the unpaid seller. If the administrator is proposing to sell or use the goods without a court order, he can no doubt be restrained by injunction. If he has in fact used them by 'hiving down' to a new company [1.05] without the court's authority he will undoubtedly be guilty of conversion. Furthermore, the supplier has the right of application to the court to deprive the administrator of his right to dispose of the goods and has, in addition, power under section 44 to complain to the Court that the conduct of the receiver has been 'unfairly prejudiced' to his interests.

What is more, if the administrator does sell goods in the possession of the company to which it has no title and secures an order of the court to do so, section 34(5) provides that:

'It shall be a condition of an order under sub-section (2) above that
(a) the net proceeds of the disposal . . . shall be applied towards discharging the sums . . . payable under the hire purchase agreement.'

This will give the supplier with a retention of title clause some priority; but it does nothing whatsoever to secure for him the contracted price of the goods. And since most insolvency practitioners flog off goods they are entitled to sell with the minimum of effort and therefore at the lowest price, it is unlikely to realise for the supplier the real value of the goods.

However, by section 34(5)(b):

'Where those proceeds are less than such amount as may be determined by the court to be the net amount which would be realised on a sale of . . . goods in the open market by a willing vendor, such sums as may be required to make good the deficiency shall be applied towards discharging the sums . . . payable under the hire-purchase agreement.'

This purports to give the right, to the supplier of goods subject to a retention of title clause, to recover the value 'in the open market by a willing vendor'. This is, of course, totally illusionary. In the first place it does not recover the contractual price of the goods, still less other outstanding current account items. In the second place, it requires expensive litigation in order to resist the administrator's application and to recover the sum due under section 34.

The Insolvency Act 1985 can therefore only be regarded as a disaster for manufacturers and suppliers, which will enable banks and financial institutions to enrich themselves at their expense. However, this will only apply when an administrator has been appointed by the court, and in all other situations a skilfully drafted retention of title clause should prevail over receivers.

Draft Retention of Title Clauses

In the current state of the law, which includes the Insolvency Act 1985, it is believed that the following terms should be effective to preserve the supplier's title to goods. However, neither the author nor the publishers warrant that they will do so or accept legal liability of any kind in respect of these suggested terms.

Goods intended for resale by the prospective purchaser substantially in the form received

The Terms of Trade of . . . . PLC/Ltd (hereinafter called 'the company')
All orders, in whatever terms, are accepted subject to the following terms and conditions which no person in the employment of or acting in any way as agent of the company, or purporting so to do, has power to vary. Previous dealings between the company and any customer shall not vary or replace these terms or be deemed in any circumstances so to do. Acceptance of the goods by a customer shall be conclusive evidence before any court of law or arbitrator that these terms apply.

The intending purchaser acknowledges that before entering into an agreement for the purchase of any goods from the company he has expressly represented and warranted that he is not insolvent and has not committed any act of bankruptcy, or, being a company with limited or unlimited liability, knows of no circumstances which would entitle any debenture holder or secured creditor to appoint a receiver, to petition for winding-up of the company or apply for the appointment of an administrator or exercise any other rights over or against the company's assets.

The Conditions:

(1) the acceptance by the company of any order for goods shall constitute an agreement to sell the goods and not be a sale of them and no title to the said goods shall pass to the intending purchaser by reason of delivery or acceptance of the same.

(2) the company shall remain the sole and absolute owner of the goods until such a time as the agreed price of the goods shall have been paid to the company by the intending purchaser. Until such time the intending purchaser shall be the bailee of the goods for the company and shall store them upon his premises separately from his own goods or those of any other person and in a manner which makes them readily identifiable as the goods of the company.

(3) goods the subject of any agreement by the company to sell shall be at the risk of the intending purchaser as soon as they are delivered by the company to his vehicles or his premises or otherwise to his order.

(4) the intending purchaser's right to possession of the goods shall cease at whichever is the earliest of the following dates:

(a) on the expiration of the agreed period of credit, if any

(b) if he, not being a company, commits an act of bankruptcy, makes a proposal to his creditors for a composition under section 110 of the Insolvency Act 1985 or does anything which would entitle a petition for a bankruptcy order to be made

(c) if the intending purchaser, being a company, does anything or fails to do anything which would entitle a receiver to take possession of any assets or which would entitle any person to present a petition for winding up or apply for an administration order.

(5) if a company, the intending purchaser or any director thereof shall not apply to the court under section 28(1) of the Insolvency Act 1985 for the appointment of an administrator without giving fourteen days' notice to the company. From the date of the said notice, the intending purchaser shall not be entitled to remain in possession of any of the company's goods. The appointment of an administrator without the aforesaid notice, shall be deemed to be a fundamental breach of contract.

(6) the company may for the purpose of recovery of its goods enter upon any premises where they are stored or where they are reasonably thought to be stored and may repossess the same.

(7) in the case of any purchaser who is not a company, the purchase price shall be payable in two instalments, namely 10% on receipt of the goods and the balance thereof at the end of such time as may be

separately agreed or in default of agreement thirty days after the delivery of the goods.

(8) the intending purchaser shall be at liberty to sell on the company's goods at any price not less than the price agreed between the company and the intending purchaser. If he sells on his own account, he shall sell as agent and bailee of the company in law and in equity and shall hold the proceeds thereof in trust for the company and shall not mingle the proceeds with other monies and shall not pay the cheque or cash therefor into an overdrawn bank account. He shall open a fiduciary account with his bankers and advise them that he holds the entire proceeds of sale to a sub-purchaser as trustee for the company and that not until payment to the company of the agreed price shall he be entitled to transfer any profit thereon to any other account. The company shall be entitled to any interest earned on the fiduciary account.

(9) if a receiver be appointed to the intending purchaser and at the time thereof the intending purchaser shall not have received the proceeds of sale, the intending purchaser or the receiver, as agent for the intending purchaser, shall assign to the company within seven days all rights against the person or persons to whom the goods have been sold.

(10) if a receiver or manager or any other person acting for the intending purchaser fails to return any goods the property of the company, the return of which has been demanded in accordance with these conditions, he shall pay the company as agreed and liquidated damages for detinue and/or conversion, treble the agreed price of the goods; and if any such person shall fail to assign to the company any rights against a third person as required by clause 6 hereof, he shall be liable to payment to the company interest thereon at the National Westminster Bank Limited base rate plus 5 per centum until the company shall receive the whole of the monies due.

(11) if a receiver or manager or any other person acting on behalf of the intending purchaser shall in any way seek to impugn the company's title to the said goods, or shall seek to claim that this conditional sale amounts to a charge on the intending purchaser's assets, he shall pay to the company as agreed and liquidated damages for slander of title, treble the agreed price of the said goods.

Goods bought to be incorporated with or in other chattels

The Terms of Trade of ....PLC/Ltd (hereinafter called 'the company') of

. . . .
. . . .

All orders, in whatever terms, are accepted subject to the following conditions which no person in the employment of or acting in any way as agent of the company, or purporting so to do, has power to vary. Previous dealings between the company and any customer shall not vary or replace these terms or be deemed in any circumstances so to do. Acceptance of the goods by a customer shall be conclusive evidence before any court of law or arbitrator that these terms apply.

The intending purchaser acknowledges that before entering into an agreement for the purchase of any goods from the company he has expressly represented and warranted that he is not insolvent and has not committed any act of bankruptcy, or being a company with limited or unlimited liability, knows of no circumstances which would entitle any debenture holder or secured creditor to appoint a receiver, to petition for winding up of the company or apply for the appointment of an administrator or exercise any other rights over or against the company's assets.

The Conditions:

(1) the acceptance by the company of any order for goods shall constitute an agreement to sell the goods and not a sale of them and no title to the said goods shall pass to the intending purchaser by reason of delivery or acceptance of the same.
(2) the company shall remain the sole and absolute owner of the goods until such a time as the agreed price of the goods have been paid to the company by the intending purchaser. Until such time the intending purchaser shall be the bailee of the goods for the company and shall store them upon his premises separately from his own goods or those of any other person and in a manner which makes them readily identifiable as the goods of the company.
(3) goods the subject of any agreement by the company to sell shall be at the risk of the intending purchaser as soon as they are delivered by the company to his vehicles or his premises or otherwise to his order
(4) the intending purchaser's right to possession of the goods shall cease at whichever is the earliest of the following dates:

    (a) on the expiration of the agreed period of credit, if any
    (b) if he, not being a company, commits an act of bankruptcy, makes a proposal to his creditors for a composition under section 110 of

the Insolvency Act 1985 or does anything which would entitle a petition for a bankruptcy order to be made

(c) if the intending purchaser, being a company, does anything or fails to do anything which would entitle a receiver to take possession of any assets or which would entitle any person to present a petition for winding up or apply for an administration order.

(5) if a company, the intending purchaser or any director thereof shall not apply to the court under section 28(1) of the Insolvency Act 1985 for the appointment of an administrator without giving fourteen days' notice to the company. From the date of the said notice, the intending purchaser shall not be entitled to remain in possession of any of the company's goods.

(6) the intending purchaser shall be at liberty to incorporate the company's goods into another product or chattel subject to the condition that if goods the property of the company are admixed or united in any way with those of the intending purchaser, the product thereof shall become and/or shall be deemed to be for all purposes to be the property of the company. If goods the property of the company are admixed or united in any way with the property of any person or persons other than the intending purchaser or are processed with or incorporated therein, the product thereof shall become and shall be deemed for all purposes to be owned in common with that other person or those other persons.

(7) on the sale to a sub-purchaser of any product, goods or chattels to which the company's goods have been attached or been incorporated, the proceeds therefor shall be held in trust for the company, shall not be mingled with other monies and shall not be paid into any overdrawn bank account but shall be paid into a fiduciary account for the company with the intending purchaser's bankers who shall be advised that the intending purchaser holds the entire proceeds of sale to a sub-purchaser as trustee for the company and not until payment to the company of the agreed price shall he be entitled to transfer any other monies to any other account. The company shall be entitled to any interest earned on the fiduciary account.

(8) if a receiver be appointed to the intending purchaser and at the time thereof the intending purchaser shall not have received the proceeds of sale, the intending purchaser or the receiver, as agent for the intending purchaser, shall assign to the company within seven days all rights against the person or persons to whom the goods have been sold.

(9) if a receiver or manager or any other person acting for the intending purchaser fails to return any goods the property of the company, the return of which has been demanded in accordance with these conditions, he shall pay the company as agreed and liquidated damages for detinue and/or conversion, treble the agreed price of the goods; and if any such person shall fail to assign to the company any rights against a third person as required by clause 6 hereof, he shall be liable to payment to the company plus interest thereon at the National Westminster Bank Limited base rate plus 5 per centum until the company shall receive the whole of the monies due.

(10) if a receiver or manager or any other person acting on behalf of the intending purchaser shall in any way seek to impugn the company's title to the said goods, or shall seek to claim that this conditional sale amounts to a charge on the intending purchaser's assets, he shall pay to the company as agreed and liquidated damages for slander of title, treble the agreed price of the said goods.

Table of Cases

Note

The following abbreviations of English Reports are used:

AC – Law Reports Appeal Cases Series
All ER – All England Law Reports
Ch – Law Reports Chancery Series
ER – English Reports
KB – Law Reports King's Bench Series
QB – Law Reports Queen's Bench Series
WLR – Weekly Law Reports

Table of Statutes

Index

Note: Numbers following entries refer to section numbers